30 MEAL PLANS FROM

Archana's
Kitchen

30 MEAL PLANS FROM

Archana's Kitchen

Easy Indian Vegetarian Recipes for Good Health

ARCHANA DOSHI

HarperCollins *Publishers* India

First published in India by HarperCollins *Publishers* 2022
4th Floor, Tower A, Building No. 10, Phase II, DLF Cyber City,
Gurugram, Haryana – 122002
www.harpercollins.co.in

2 4 6 8 10 9 7 5 3 1

P-ISBN: 978-93-9440-768-8
E-ISBN: 978-93-9440-776-3

Typeset in 11/14 Adobe Garamond at
Manipal Technologies Limited, Manipal

Printed and bound at
Thomson Press (India) Ltd

MIX
Paper
FSC® C010615

This book is produced from independently certified FSC® paper
to ensure responsible forest management.

To
My dad, who taught me to explore and enjoy every moment of life to the fullest

Contents

Accompaniments

Introduction

'Archana, come whip the butter and sugar!' My mom would pull me into the kitchen whenever she was in the mood to bake something—and I would have no choice but to follow her. But don't get me wrong—I loved every minute of it. The tasks that were assigned to me were basic: whether it was beating together sugar and butter, using a wooden ladle, until I had a creamy batter for the softest Victoria sponge cake, or thinly slicing nuts for garnishing desserts or even making whipped cream icing for cakes. Baking was my first step in my now long journey of making food. For every kitchen task, I was my mother's little assistant.

However, I wasn't alone in carrying out my kitchen duties. My mother didn't believe that the kitchen was only a place for girls or women, so my brother often accompanied us. And today we are a family that loves to cook. My brother equally loves cooking and whipping up new and old dishes. By the time I was twelve years old, I was whipping up entire meals by myself. From rasam to poriyal to rice to even making the perfect roti and dosa, I had quite a culinary repertoire. By the age of fifteen, I was making the most delicious French gateau. It sounds like boasting, but I simply loved eating my own cake! Till date there has never been a day when I have cooked a meal and not licked my own plate clean!

I live to eat. Food tickles my enthusiasm and when I eat someone else's food, I like to anticipate flavours and textures. I also love feeding people. I often host parties and invite friends and family to try out new cuisines and dishes. Cooking brings me a sense of calm and peace like no other activity.

I worked as a software engineer for a few years in the initial part of my career and lost my job in the 2001 dot-com burst. It was then I started to think: what was my journey going to be for the next decade or more of my life? My mind was itching to do something on my own, related to food and good health. I became a yoga teacher, but my friends were convinced that I needed to do something with food. They also complained that most cookbooks were difficult, and they never got the desired result or that dishes they cooked from the recipes never tasted as great as they looked in the pictures. So, cooking to them was not a fun activity. I know many folks who feel similarly. I wanted to break this mindset. I wanted to make cooking fun and easy by using simple cooking techniques that employ fresh, local ingredients. So, I started testing and writing down my recipes and Archana's Kitchen was born in November 2007. Today, it is India's leading food and recipe platform which actively promotes healthy cooking and mindful eating.

This book will make you fall in love with cooking and food. There is a difference between cooking yummy food and cooking delicious yet healthy food. The former can be achieved easily, with the overuse of taste-enhancing ingredients like butter and ghee. However, as someone who is passionate about food, I also care deeply about how eating food affects our bodies. I truly believe we are what we eat, and that our health is largely decided by what we put on the table.

As part of practising mindful eating, my mission was to return to the basics of cooking food that ensures a healthy body, mind and soul. While my website empowers people to cook food easily in the kitchen even if they have limited preparation time, it has also been a source of knowledge for me. I have been listening to users who are confused about pairing foods to get the best nutritional value without compromising on taste. And the more I listen to them, the more I realize that there is a big problem that most users are facing: people are gaining weight, becoming sicker and suffering from lifestyle-related issues from a young age. Most of these issues are related to the *quantity* and *quality* of food we are eating today, along with other lifestyle disturbances such as lack of restful sleep, always being connected to technology and not taking quality time off. These trends disturb me deeply and I want to bring about a change. This book is my way of helping people plan easy, everyday meals that will ensure a balanced diet.

How to Use This Book

The ideal meal should be a balanced one, featuring all the main food groups. In this book, I have curated thirty meal plans which feature a combination of carbohydrates (rice or roti or millets), protein (dals, vegetables, beans), vitamins and minerals (vegetables), and probiotics (curd, lassi). I have tried to focus on keeping the meal plans wholesome and spread across various regional Indian cuisines so that it is appealing and accessible to anyone across the country.

Some of the meals also mix and match cuisines to make a fun fusion experience. I believe that food should be fun and that there is no harm in experimenting. Although each meal plan is complete in itself, don't hesitate to mix and match recipes from different plans.

Go through the meal plans on the Contents page and pick a plan or recipe to suit your needs. Before you begin cooking, do make sure you have read through the entire recipe first—the ingredients list will help you with preparation, the method will give you an idea of the vessels you need as well as how to optimize the process of cooking the dish, and thus, save your time!

The Important Food Groups

Protein

- Proteins are essential building blocks that help the body build and repair tissue, muscles, cartilage and skin, as well as pump blood.
- Vegetarian proteins can be in the form of whole dals, paneer, tofu, chana, rajma, milk, dahi, green vegetables or sprouts.

- Having one helping of a protein-based dish with every meal is essential for maintaining good health. Protein-rich foods help you keep fuller for longer, helps you feel satiated, and thus, you are less likely to get hunger pangs during the interim between meals.

Fats

- There are good fats and bad fats, and many people tend to avoid any food that is fatty. As a general principle, it is a good thing to restrict fat intake, but our bodies require a certain amount of dietary fats to gain body energy and to support cell growth, synthesize hormones, store vitamins, and much more.

- A diet must consist of healthy fats—polyunsaturated, monounsaturated and omega-3 fatty acids. Using restricted quantities of ghee, mustard oil, coconut oil, sesame oil, groundnut oil, sunflower oil or even rice bran oil is the optimal way to consume fats. In addition, there are many foods we already eat—paneer, milk, curd, etc.—all of which contain good fats that are important for our diet.

- But do avoid deep-fried foods and highly processed foods which contain a lot of trans fat.

- Once again, you must exercise portion control in the amount of healthy and unhealthy fats you eat. If curd is healthy, it does not mean you should live on a curd diet and eat more than your body can take. If ghee is good for you, it does not mean you cook in ghee and eat only ghee-rich foods. Eating all fats in the right portions is extremely important. And that portion is something you can determine based on your body type, your health requirements and the suggestions given by your nutritionist or doctor.

Carbohydrates

- Carbohydrates are one of the main sources of energy.
- It is important to choose and eat the right kind of carbs. Avoid carb-rich processed foods like bread and biscuits which are known to be simple carbohydrates. When making rotis or parathas, make

your atta multigrain by adding flours made out of ragi, jowar, bajra, etc., which are whole grain flours that contain complex carbohydrates.

- If you are a rice-eater, then opt for brown rice or millets which have more fibre and nutrition than white rice. If you are making dosa batter, then add millets like ragi, bajra, jowar, etc., to increase your fibre content.

- Adding fibre-rich carbohydrates that are packed with nutrients to your diet helps slow the digestion process and keeps you feeling full for longer.

Vitamins, Minerals, Fibre

- Vitamins and minerals, especially Vitamins A, E, B12, D, calcium, zinc, magnesium, and iron, are essential for the body. Vitamins and minerals help in better metabolism, muscle function, bone health and cell production.

- It's important to include a good portion of fruits, vegetables, green leafy vegetables, colourful salads, nuts and dry fruits throughout the day either in your meal or when you snack.

- Include lots of raw vegetables in the form of salads in at least two meals. Indian salads are great because they are simple and quick to make and can be made tasty and chatpata with locally available ingredients. Adding raw vegetables and fruits in your diet will also ensure you get the adequate fibre that your body needs to stay healthy.

Eating Mindfully

Being mindful is an exercise with manifold returns. Our lives are fast-paced and demanding, and more often than not we tend to forget the most important parts of our day—which are our meal and snack times. We eat our meals in front of our laptop or grab something for lunch while multitasking. If we don't pay attention to what or how we are eating, how can we measure the nutrition that our bodies require?

Food is our fuel. I believe that if we eat all the foods we love in moderation, and mindfully, we will be on a path to exactly the space where we want to live the rest of our lives. This means that you can eat your puri, paratha, kheer or halwa but do so in portioned quantities along with mindful eating practices. Of course, if you suffer from a particular illness, it's best to follow your doctor's advice and avoid foods that they have recommended against.

Mindful Eating Practices

Stop eating when you feel full: Our bodies are a great indicator of our hunger quotient. Eat when you are hungry and stop when your body says it's full or is getting full. It is vital to pay attention to your portion size when watching your diet as well.

Eat slowly, without distractions: Eating slowly is often ignored when we sit down for a meal, especially when we are in a hurry, rushing to school or work or having lunch at the office desk or at a restaurant. When there is a lot of food on the table, or when there is a lot of work on our minds, we tend to eat fast and, in the process, forget about how much we are eating. Most of us eat much faster than the time it takes for our gut to send a signal to the brain that it is full.[1] Slowing down your eating tempo will give your gut enough time to send signals to your brain. Chewing well and eating slowly also helps in better digestion. On the other hand, eating quickly leads to poor digestion, increased weight gain, and lower levels of satisfaction, leading to the feeling that we have not eaten enough.

---

1 Ann MacDonald, 'Why Eating Slowly May Help You Feel Full Faster', Harvard Health Publishing, 19 October 2010, https://www.health.harvard.edu/blog/ why-eating-slowly-may-help-you-feel-full-faster-20101019605; Ruairi Robertson, 'The Gut-Brain Connection: How It Works and the Role of Nutrition', Healthline, 20 August 2020, https://www.healthline.com/nutrition/gut-brain-connection.

Turn off the TV and keep your phone away: A great way to be mindful about what goes into your body is to keep mobile phones, TV, books, newspapers and other miscellaneous distractions out of your sight when you are eating. This helps you focus on what's on your plate and practise portion control and mindful eating.

Lay out the dinner table: If you are at home, ensure that you have a well-laid-out table with plates and spoons, and that the food is portioned in small serving bowls. These tips help bring mindfulness into what you eat and how much you eat. Your focus is on your food and the time you spend with your family (if you are eating together). These small rituals help make eating a pleasurable affair.

At the office: If you are at work on your desk, then closing your laptop and keeping your phone facedown will help you focus on the food in your lunch box. Having fewer distractions will not only shift your focus back to the food you are going to eat, but it will also help you be in the moment with friends and colleagues.

Eat local, eat seasonal: Eating healthy begins at home. Our humble rotis, dal, sabzi, sambar, rasam, kootu, curry, poriyal, palya, kuzhambu, saaru, chutney, dahi, chaas, pickle, etc., contain all the essentials foundations to a well-balanced diet. Turn your focus inwards, to your home, rather than out.

Add colour, texture and variety to your meal plan: A great way to plan a meal is to cook a variety of dishes that add colour to your plate. Your plate should look colourful and include foods from the various groups. This ensures your body is getting adequate nutrition.

What Is Portion Control?

When human babies are born and begin feeding, they are known to eat when they are hungry and stop feeding when they feel full. But as we grow up, we tend to be exposed to a lot more food, fad diets, irregular mealtimes, work pressure, stress, lack of exercise, etc. Our eating habits have changed dramatically in recent times with the availability of ready-to-eat foods in the market. In addition, our increasingly fast-paced lifestyles encourage us to lean on highly processed foods like pizza, chips, biscuits, desserts and aerated drinks.

We can say that this kind of 'junk eating' is due to the lack of time to prepare fresh food for ourselves and because we have easy access to these foods and snacks. It is hard to avoid such foods in our everyday lifestyle, but what is possible is to understand how we can moderate the consumption of such processed foods by exercising portion control in our daily meals. There is plenty of research[2] on how large portion sizes can have an impact on health.

It took me many years of practice to unlearn certain eating habits—the first one being overeating. I often found myself unable to stop even when I was full because my tongue loved the chatpata taste of, let's say, the chaat I was eating. In much of India, our families and friends are often offended if we eat small quantities; they assume that we don't like the food they've made for us. So, they try to force us to eat till we are stuffed. Today, I can proudly say that my entire family understands that it is okay not to eat when you are not hungry, and it is okay to stop eating if you are feeling full. As long as we balance our nutritional needs through the day, we'll be fine.

To effect change, the key is to change the way we snack and eat our everyday meals *mindfully*, keeping portion sizes in the forefront of our minds. Of course, this does not in any way mean that we should rely on easy junk food every day. Eating a well-balanced diet is the cornerstone of good health. But when we consistently overeat, even if it's healthy food, it tends to leave us feeling a bit tired and sluggish, and eventually over time it spells disaster for our weight and health.

When it comes to keeping good health, losing weight—or even fighting lifestyle-related diseases like diabetes, hypertension, high

---

2 'Do Increased Portion Sizes Affect How Much We Eat?' Research to Practice Series, No. 2 (May 2006), Centers for Disease Control and Prevention, https://www.cdc.gov/nccdphp/dnpa/nutrition/pdf/portion_size_research.pdf.

cholesterol, and more—consistently eating the right portion sizes, which includes adding the right food groups in our diet, plays an important role.

Portion control, along with mindful eating, is one of the core essences of good nutrition. It is not about losing weight or counting calories. It is about focusing on developing a healthy relationship between the food we eat and our bodies. I should add that some form of daily exercise, be it regular walks, yoga or strength training, is a must in our routine.

The Katori Diet for Portion Control

A portion is the amount of food you serve on your plate. It can be hard to measure every portion of the food you eat, but there are some simple ways to know if you are eating the right portion sizes.

A great way to practise portion control is something I like to call the 'katori diet'. This is something most Indians are familiar with because it was the way we ate traditionally. I have personally been practising for this for years.

In this method, we use regular, small-sized katoris at home. Most often, a typical Indian meal will have one sabzi, one dal, one roti, a small katori of rice, a salad like kachumber and chaas/dahi. This makes a great meal. If you are doing this already, then you are halfway there. If you prefer not to use katoris to portion these items, you can even go out and get yourself a thali or a slotted plate. One thali will usually have a larger area and three smaller slots. Carbs like rotis and rice go into the larger area, while the other three slots are allotted to various food groups like veggies, dal, salad, etc. Along with this there are servings of pickle and papad. This method is a great way to measure out the portions of your food. One helping is usually enough for the average Indian body type.

Kitchen Essentials

When I started cooking in my own kitchen, there were many things I had to collect to have a good cooking experience. I began with a few plates and serving bowls and one or two cooking pots and pans. I lived out of packets of spices stuck into refrigerator doors for a few years but not for long.

Cooking can be a therapeutic and meditative experience, and once you have a well-organized pantry with your staples packed in bottles and canisters, the cooking experience becomes enjoyable. Today, my kitchen has a well-stocked pantry with spices and ingredients and sauces from around the world. I have also collected various sizes of pots, pans and kadais to suit my various cooking needs and techniques.

In the list below, I have shared the basic utensils and tools that you should try to introduce into your kitchen collection because they make life so much easier when you want to whip up a meal. The list is not expansive, but it'll get you far. If you are new to cooking, it's not necessary to go out and buy everything. Start with the basics and as you grow in your culinary journey, you can invest in more items based on your requirements.

Pots, Pans and Tools for an Indian Kitchen

Pressure Cookers

Pressure cookers are a godsend. They are adaptive and quick and can be used to make everything from rice, dal and beans to biryanis and other one-pot dishes. It's always good to have these in at least three sizes. In terms of material, the hard anodized pressure cookers are perfect for cooking directly in the pot and easy to maintain as well.

2 litres: perfect for steaming and cooking vegetables and potatoes

3 litres: perfect for cooking dal, rice and similar items for a family of four

5 litres: ideal when you want to make food for a large gathering

Pots and Pans

Stir-Fry Pans: Great for roasting and stir-fry cooking. These pans can be of iron or stainless-steel material. In certain cases where you would like to make dishes crispy with less oil, a good quality non-stick will be useful. You should ideally have one of each size—with a pan diameter of 20 cm and 25 to 30 cm.

Saucepans: Great for making chai and sauces, soups and other curry-based dishes.

You should ideally have two pans—2 litre and another 5 litre one with two side handles.

Wok/Kadai: Perfect for stir frying dishes from vegetables to noodles to fried rice.

Iron kadais are usually better and bring out the flavour of dishes. You should aim to have two—one for deep frying and a larger one for stir frying.

Steamers: Great for making steamed dishes like idlis, modaks, etc.

If you have an idli or dhokla cooker, you don't need a separate steamer because these do the job perfectly.

Tawas/Skillets: Iron tawas are great for making phulkas and parathas. They can also be used for making dosa. However, ensure you maintain two separate tawas for dosa and roti/paratha. Irons pans for dosa require regular greasing and maintenance before they are used, so whenever you are making dosas on a well-seasoned tawa, it will not stick to the pan and will come out easily.

It's always good to have a good quality non-stick tawa at home as well. It helps in making dishes faster and with less oil.

Paniyaram Pan: Great for frying small portions while using less oil. A paniyaram pan has cavities which makes it easy to pan fry small portions of food like muffins, frittatas, paniyaram, pakoras, kofta and vadas. The number of cavities varies for different pan sizes. A cast iron paniyaram pan requires more oil to fry, whereas the non-stick version requires very little oil.

Grill Pan: Great to make sandwiches, tikkas and grilled vegetables. Easy to use and without the fuss of charcoal, these pans are perfect for making snacks. Cast iron grill pans are a great investment because they will last you a lifetime.

Tadka Pan: An essential item for Indian seasonings.

No Indian kitchen should be without a tadka pan. Tadka is an Indian technique of cooking seasonings and spices separately in oil or ghee and then adding it to the main curry or dal. Using a small pan like this also helps you use less oil/ghee. Hard anodized pans are a great material and very easy to clean and maintain, too.

Other Essentials

Mortar and Pestle: This is one my favourite kitchen tools because it is the quickest way to grind small quantities of spices. Choose one that is wide or with a high wall. Marble or stone would be your best friend when you a plan to buy a pestle and mortar.

Chakla–Belan Set: Important for making rotis, parathas and other Indian breads. They come in different materials like marble, wood and stainless steel. I personally prefer marble, as it's sturdy and long-lasting. Make sure you look for a stable board. Sometimes the grooves will be slippery and keep moving as you roll. The best ones are the heavier ones because they will be more stable.

Must-Have Cooking Tools

- Pakad (pot-holder)
- Potato masher
- Lemon squeezer
- Chimta/tongs
- Whisk
- Bottle/tin-opener
- Tea strainer

- Grater
- Pot lids/covers
- Slotted spoon for deep frying
- Flat spatula for cooking parathas, cheela, etc., in wood and stainless steel
- Flat and scooped serving spoons. The flat ones are great for sabzi and rice and the scooped versions for dal, rasam, sambar, kadhi, soups or anything that is of a liquid consistency. Try to have at least two pairs of this set. I have five pairs (ten of each) at home, as I cook multiple dishes and have guests often and hence, I am not scrambling to serve at mealtime.

Pantry and Seasonal Vegetables

Your pantry should always be stocked with essentials like spices, dals, sauces, condiments and flavouring agents from various cuisines. I love to stock different types of lentils and legumes, as well as items for breakfast like poha, sooji, broken rice, broken wheat, etc. If I need to whip up something even if there is no vegetable in the refrigerator, there will be something in the pantry which I can use to put a meal together. As you begin exploring various cuisines and start favouring one or the other, you will, over time, build up your personalized pantry essentials.

For Indian cuisine, the basics include:

- Basic regional rice varieties like basmati rice, sona masuri, ponni raw rice, gobind bhog rice, Kerala matta rice, etc.
- Whole grain flours: whole wheat flour and millet flours like jowar, ragi, bajra, barley, gram flour, etc.
- Lentils and legumes: these can be used in combinations of whole and split, based on your preference. Try to stock up on varieties like moong dal, urad dal, horse gram, masoor dal, rajma, kala chana, kabuli chana, black-eyed beans, etc.
- Seasoning essentials like mustard seeds, cumin seeds, methi seeds, til seeds, khus khus, split urad dal, etc.

- Spice powders and condiments like turmeric powder, coriander powder, cumin powder, garam masala, sambar powder, red chilli powder, black pepper powder, cardamom powder, cinnamon powder, kala namak, etc.
- Whole spices and dry herbs like cinnamon, cardamom, badi elaichi, cloves, dry cumin, black peppercorns, Kashmiri chillies, kasuri methi, saffron, etc.
- Regional spice mixes such as chana masala, pav bhaji masala, panch phoran, goda masala, etc.
- Fresh herbs that can be kept refrigerated such as coriander leaves, curry leaves, mint leaves, methi leaves, etc.
- Other essentials include poha, sooji, raw and roasted peanuts, broken rice, broken wheat, sabudana, freshly grated coconut, coconut milk, assorted nuts and dry fruits for garnishing, etc.

As for vegetables, it is a good idea to cook seasonal vegetables because they always taste better when in season. Peas will taste sweeter in the winter months while the family of gourd vegetables will be juicier during the summer months. My fridge looks absolutely colourful all year round. I buy all the basics from carrots, radish, cucumbers, green chillies, ginger and essential herbs like coriander and mint to fancier items like purple cabbage, broccoli and amaranth.

Another essential that my kitchen is never without when I am cooking, especially in the evenings, is some lovely music. It brings in good vibes and makes cooking a magical experience.

30 MEAL PLANS

MEAL PLAN 1

What's on the Plate?

- Huli Soppu Saaru (Tangy Curry with Fresh Greens)
- Badanekayi Palya (Crunchy and Spicy Green Brinjal Stir Fry)
- Methi Carrot Jowar Thepla (Fenugreek Leaf Carrot Spiced Millet Bread)
- Tomato Onion Cucumber Raita (Vegetables in Spiced Curd; p. 149)
- Rice with Ghee

This delectable protein and vitamin-rich south Indian inspired meal consists of huli soppu saaru that is made with toor dal and freshly ground spices. When you serve it along with a brinjal vegetable known as badanekayi palya, the millet-rich methi thepla, a fibre-packed raita and half a katori of rice topped with ghee, it makes a wholesome and nutritious meal.

Alternatively, you can skip the rice and serve this with hot phulkas. In addition, grate some carrots into the raita to amp up the nutrition.

Huli Soppu Saaru

Saaru means a curry or a sambar in which dal is combined with greens like amaranth, spinach or methi leaves, with freshly ground spices to lend an aromatic flavour to the dish. If you are pressed for time, you

1

can use pre-made sambar powder instead of roasting and grinding the fresh masala. It will taste just as lovely.

Ingredients

1 cup toor dal
½ tsp turmeric powder
30 gm tamarind, soaked in hot water
250 gm amaranth greens, chopped
100 gm methi leaves, chopped
Salt to taste

For the roasted saaru powder

1 tbsp chana dal (Bengal gram dal)
2 tsp split white urad dal
2 tbsp coriander seeds
1 tsp methi seeds
4 dry red chillies
2 tsp cumin seeds
1 tsp whole black peppercorns
2 tbsp fresh coconut, grated

For the seasoning

1 tsp ghee
½ tsp mustard seeds
½ tsp cumin seeds
2 dry red chillies, broken
1 sprig curry leaves, torn
¼ tsp asafoetida
1 cup baby onions (sambar onions), peeled and halved
1 tsp jaggery

Method

Wash the toor dal and add it to the pressure cooker with 2½ cups of water and turmeric powder. Cover the cooker and pressure cook for 2 whistles on medium heat. After 2 whistles, turn the heat to low and simmer for 3 to 4 minutes and turn off the heat. Allow the pressure to release naturally. Once the pressure has released, open the cooker and mash the dal lightly until smooth.

Soak the tamarind in hot water for 15 minutes. Then, using your fingers, mash the tamarind well into the water until it feels completely soft. This process helps to extract the juice and sourness from the tamarind. Repeat this process a couple of times by adding ¼ cup of water at a time. Sieve the tamarind water into a single bowl and set aside.

Next, add the chopped amaranth and methi leaves to the pressure cooker with ½ tsp salt. Add 2 tbsp of water and pressure cook for 2 whistles on high heat and turn off the heat. Release the pressure immediately by lifting the weight with a fork. Releasing the pressure immediately ensures the greens retain their bright colour. Keep aside.

Preheat a pan over medium heat; add the chana dal and urad dal and roast until the dals turn golden and lightly crisp. Add the coriander seeds, cumin seeds, methi seeds, black pepper and dry red chillies. Stir for another minute or two until the seeds start crackling and you can smell the aromas coming through. Finally, add the coconut and stir it for 30 to 40 seconds and turn off the heat. Allow the mixture to cool. Once cool, blend to make a fine powder. Keep aside.

Next, make the saaru. Heat the ghee in a large saucepan over medium heat; add the mustard seeds, cumin and red chillies and allow the seeds to splutter. Add the curry leaves, asafoetida and the baby onions. Sauté the baby onions until they turn soft and translucent. Then, add the tamarind water, jaggery and the roasted masala powder. Give the mixture a stir and simmer the tamarind mixture for 3 to 4 minutes until the raw taste goes away.

After 3 to 4 minutes, add the cooked dal and the cooked greens to the tamarind gravy. Give it a stir, add salt to taste and bring the Huli Soppu Saaru to a brisk boil for 2 to 3 minutes and turn off the heat. Check the salt and adjust it according to your taste. Transfer to a serving bowl.

Badanekayi Palya

This is a delightful side dish made with long green brinjals, but you can use any brinjal of your choice. The freshly ground spices, along with the crunchy masala of roasted peanuts and sesame seeds, makes this brinjal dish stand out. Perfect to go with hot phulkas, too, or simply mix it along with hot steamed rice topped with ghee.

Ingredients

6-8 long green brinjal or small purple ones, cut into 1-inch pieces
½ tsp mustard seeds
1 sprig curry leaves, torn
1 onion, finely chopped
1 tomato, finely chopped
1 tsp turmeric powder
1 tbsp sambar powder
2 tbsp jaggery
Salt to taste
1 to 2 tbsp sesame oil for cooking

For roasting

¼ cup shelled roasted peanuts
¼ cup sesame seeds

Method

Place the cut brinjal in a bowl of water to prevent discolouration.

In a small pan, add the roasted peanuts and sesame seeds and roast them for about a minute on medium heat or until you notice that the sesame seeds are beginning to crackle. Turn off the heat and set aside to cool. Once cool, add this to the small jar of your mixer-grinder and blend to make a coarse powder.

Heat oil in a large stir fry pan over medium heat; add the mustard seeds and allow them to splutter. Add the chopped onion and curry leaves and sauté until the onions soften and turn translucent.

Once done, add the tomato and sauté until it becomes slightly soft. Stir in the turmeric powder.

Drain the water from the cut brinjals and add it to the tomato–onion mixture. Sprinkle salt and give it a gentle stir. Cover the pan and cook the brinjals on medium heat until they turn soft. This will take about 4 to 5 minutes. Ensure you stir it a couple of times in between.

Finally, stir in the sambar powder, jaggery, and the roasted peanuts and sesame seeds powder.

Check the salt and add more, if needed, to taste. Stir fry the brinjal in the open pan for another couple of minutes until the masala is well combined with the brinjal. Once done, turn off the heat and transfer to a serving bowl and serve hot.

∽

Carrot Methi Jowar Thepla

Theplas are perfectly flavoured Indian breads that go with almost any sabzi. In traditional Gujarati cuisine, theplas are made with methi leaves. In this recipe, I have packed in additional flavours and nutrition by adding grated carrots and by using the mineral-rich jowar flour. This thepla can be a meal on its own. You can have it for breakfast with a chutney or pickle or even pack it for your travels.

Ingredients

    2 carrots, grated
    1 cup methi leaves, finely chopped
    1½ cups jowar flour
    1 cup whole wheat flour
    1 tsp red chilli powder
    ½ tsp turmeric powder
    2 tsp cumin powder
    Salt to taste
    Oil for cooking

Method

In a large mixing bowl, add the grated carrot, chopped methi leaves, turmeric powder, red chilli powder, cumin powder, salt, whole wheat flour and jowar flour.

Add water, a little at a time, and knead to make a soft, smooth dough which is not sticky. Drizzle a little oil on top and knead until smooth. Divide the dough into equal lemon-size portions and keep aside.

Preheat a pan over medium heat. Dust the dough portions with flour and roll gently to make a 6-inch diameter circle. Theplas are usually rolled thin and cooked fast on a pan. So roll it as thin as you are comfortable rolling.

Place the rolled thepla gently on the tawa and cook on both sides. Drizzle oil and cook till the thepla has brown spots on both sides. Cook on high heat as the theplas are thin and get cooked quickly.

Stack the cooked theplas one over the other. The stacking helps to retain the softness and ensures they can be served any time of the day without reheating.

MEAL PLAN 2

What's on the Plate?

- Nawabi Kofta Curry (Dry Fruit Stuffed Cottage Cheese in Creamy Tomato Gravy)
- Rajasthani Kadhi (Garlic-Flavoured Soupy Yogurt Curry)
- Paneer Pulao (Spiced Rice with Cottage Cheese)
- Boondi Raita (Chickpea Flour Bits in Yogurt; p. 148)
- Jowar Atta Roti (Sorghum Flatbread, p. 152)
- Lacha Pyaz (Pickled Onions; p. 155)
- Jhat Pat Mirchi (Stir-Fried Green Chillies; p. 158)

Weekends are times when my family looks forward to extra-special meals. Here is one of our favorite meals which is a perfect marriage of dishes from north India. The dry fruit stuffed nawabi kofta curry paired with Rajasthani kadhi, jowar atta roti, pulao and the accompaniments will, no doubt, leave you feeling warm and nourished. This makes a perfect meal for those breezy monsoon days or chilly winters.

This meal plan is packed with proteins, nutrition and flavour. You'll have to exercise self-restraint and be cautious to serve yourself sensible-sized small portions, because this delicious combination of foods will keep you coming back for more. It is during meals like this that we practise mindful eating.

∾

Nawabi Kofta Curry

A rich and delectable curry of dry fruit stuffed paneer koftas in a creamy, spicy tomato gravy. The best part is that the koftas are not deep fried; instead, they are made in a paniyaram pan to retain their nutritional value. A paniyaram pan is a traditional south Indian cooking vessel made of cast iron. The surface is dotted with cavities, which makes it super easy to cook koftas in it with less oil.

Ingredients

For the koftas

   4 boiled and mashed potatoes
   2 tbsp gram flour
   1 tsp black pepper powder
   1 cup crumbled paneer
   2 green chillies, finely chopped
   1 tsp cumin powder
   1 tsp garam masala powder
   A handful of coriander leaves, finely chopped
   2 tbsp cashew nuts, finely chopped
   2 tbsp raisins, finely chopped
   Salt to taste

For the kofta curry

   2 tbsp ghee
   2 cups tomato puree
   2 onions, roughly chopped

5 cloves garlic
1-inch ginger,
½ tsp turmeric powder
1 tsp Kashmiri red chilli powder
1 tsp jaggery
3 tbsp fresh cream
Salt to taste
A handful of coriander leaves, finely chopped

For the masala mix

1 tsp fennel seeds
1 tsp coriander seeds
2 cloves
1-inch cinnamon stick
2 cardamom pods

Method

In a large bowl, combine the mashed potatoes with the gram flour, salt and pepper powder. Mix well to make a smooth mixture. Grease your palms with a little oil and divide the mixture into 8 to 10 equal portions, and shape them into balls. Ensure that the balls are the right size so that after they are filled, they will fit into a paniyaram pan for pan frying.

To make the kofta filling, combine the crumbled paneer, cashew nuts, raisins, green chillies, salt, cumin powder, garam masala powder and coriander leaves in a bowl. Mix well. Grease your palms with a little oil and divide the mixture into 8 to 10 equal portions, shaped into tiny balls.

Once again grease your fingers and palms with oil. Take one portion of the potato mixture and flatten it on the palm of your hand. Place the paneer and dry fruit filling in the centre. Then, bring the edges of the flattened potato mixture towards the centre to cover the filling, forming a stuffed aloo kofta. Proceed similarly to make the rest of the koftas.

On medium heat, preheat a paniyaram pan with a teaspoon of oil in each cavity.

Once the oil is hot, gradually lower the koftas into each cavity, then flip and cook until golden brown all over. Drain them on an absorbent kitchen towel and set aside.

Next, make the gravy for the kofta curry. In a small skillet, dry roast the fennel seeds, coriander seeds, cloves, cinnamon and cardamom for about 3 to 4 minutes on medium heat or until the aroma of the spices waft in the air. Turn off the heat, and allow the spices to cool. Transfer the spices into a mixer jar and grind into a coarse powder, and then set aside.

In a mixer jar, combine the onions, garlic and ginger, and grind them to make a smooth paste.

Heat ghee in a heavy bottomed pan; add the freshly ground onion paste and sauté on medium heat for about 4 to 6 minutes. Add in the freshly ground spice mix and stir until you get the aroma from the spices.

Stir in the turmeric powder and chilli powder and sauté for another couple of minutes.

Add the tomato puree, salt and jaggery, and simmer until the curry is bubbling and has a delicious aromatic gravy. Add in the fresh cream and a little water if the gravy seems dry, and simmer for a few more minutes and turn off the heat.

When you are ready to serve, heat the curry. Then, place the koftas over the hot curry, garnish with coriander leaves and serve hot.

Rajasthani Kadhi

Kadhi is a classic curd-based curry which makes the perfect accompaniment for almost any meal. You can also drink warm kadhi from a bowl when you're feeling under the weather. It works like a soup and can instantly make you feel satiated. From the crushed garlic and smacking hot green chillies, to the nourishing ghee tadka, this Rajasthani kadhi is a blend of delectable flavours. During lazy days, we would just have a simple meal of kadhi along with cooked foxtail millets and vegetable stir fry or salad.

Ingredients

For the kadhi

2 tbsp gram flour
1 cup curd
¼ tsp turmeric powder
¼ tsp red chilli powder
5 cloves garlic, crushed
2 green chillies, finely chopped
Salt to taste
3 cups water

For the tadka

1 tbsp ghee
½ tsp mustard seeds
½ tsp fenugreek seeds
4 cloves
¼ tsp asafoetida
2 dry red chillies
1 sprig curry leaves, torn

Method

Make a coarse paste of garlic and green chilli by crushing them in a mortar and pestle. Chopping them will help to make the paste faster. Keep aside.

In a saucepan, combine the curd and gram flour, and whisk until smooth. Stir in the crushed green chilli and garlic, with turmeric powder, red chilli powder and salt. Add 3 cups of water and whisk the kadhi mixture well until smooth.

Place the saucepan on medium heat and bring the kadhi to a boil. Ensure you keep whisking the kadhi throughout the process. The whisking process is extremely important in order to ensure that the kadhi is of a smooth texture and that there is no curdling. Continue to whisk and boil the kadhi until the mixture is smooth. At this stage, turn the heat to low and simmer the kadhi for about 10 minutes, uncovered, and keep stirring it once in a while to keep the texture smooth.

While the kadhi is simmering, prepare the tadka.

Heat ghee in a tadka pan over medium heat. Add the mustard seeds, fenugreek seeds and cloves and allow them to splutter. Then, add asafoetida, dry red chillies and curry leaves and stir fry for a few seconds. Turn off the heat.

Add this tadka to the simmering kadhi and continue to boil it for about 5 minutes. Once it is well mixed, turn off the heat. Transfer the kadhi to a serving bowl and serve hot.

Paneer Pulao

When basmati rice is cooked in ghee with whole spices, it lends a delicious and rich flavour to a pulao. The addition of fresh mint leaves and the delicate blend of spices makes this pulao the perfect companion for a curry like kofta, kadhi or even a simple dal tadka.

Ingredients

1 cup basmati rice, washed and soaked
1½ cups water
2 onions, thinly sliced
6 cloves garlic, finely chopped
2 green chillies, slit lengthwise
2 green cardamom pods
4 cloves
1 bay leaf
2 tbsp ghee
Salt to taste
¼ cup mint leaves, roughly chopped

To stir fry

1 tbsp ghee
200 gm paneer, cut into cubes
¼ cup green peas, steamed

Method

In a large pan, heat the ghee over medium heat.

Stir in the garlic, onion and green chillies with the cardamom, clove and bay leaf. Sauté until the onions turn translucent and are slightly golden brown.

Once done, add the rice with 1½ cups of water and salt. Allow the water to come to a rolling boil. Cover the pan and turn the heat to low. Cook the pulao on low heat until all the water is absorbed and the rice is cooked through. This will take approximately 12 to 15 minutes. When all the water is absorbed and the rice is cooked, turn off the heat and keep the pan covered for 5 minutes. This will help make the rice fluffy.

Heat the ghee in a skillet on medium heat. Add the paneer cubes and sauté for about a minute. Then, add the steamed green peas and salt. Toss the paneer with the peas for a few seconds on high heat and turn off the heat.

Stir the paneer, green peas and the mint leaves into the pulao. Transfer the pulao to a serving platter and serve warm.

MEAL PLAN 3

What's on the Plate?

- Valor Muthia nu Shaak (Broad Beans Eggplant Ṣtir Fry with Fenugreek Leaf Dumplings)
- Bengali Cholar Dal (Bengali-Style Lentils)
- Puran Poli (Lentil Stuffed Indian Bread Sweetened with Jaggery)
- Curd

I often love to combine cuisines and pair dishes that make a surprising combination. Valor muthia nu shaak is a classic Gujarati dish in which broad beans and brinjal are tossed in a masala along with methi leaf dumplings. This, paired with a lip-smacking cholar dal, which has a crunch from dried coconut pieces, and served along with puran poli, makes a wholesome, protein-packed meal.

Valor Muthia nu Shaak

This Gujarati delicacy is made from flat beans (valor) and brinjal cooked with tomatoes and spices and tossed with fenugreek leaf dumplings (muthia). If you don't find valor, you can use any locally available flat beans. And 'Shaak' is the Gujarati word for a vegetable dish.

Ingredients

300 gm flat green beans, cut into ½-inch pieces
4 small brinjal, sliced into wedges
½ tsp ajwain
½ tsp mustard seeds
1-inch ginger, finely chopped
4 cloves garlic, finely chopped
2 tomatoes, finely chopped
¼ tsp asafoetida
1 tsp turmeric powder
1 tsp coriander powder
½ tsp cumin powder
1 tsp red chilli powder
1 tsp jaggery
1 tsp oil
Salt to taste

For the methi muthia (fenugreek dumplings)

50 gm methi leaves, finely chopped
¼ cup gram flour
2 tbsp whole wheat flour
½ tsp turmeric powder
1 tsp jaggery

¼ tsp asafoetida
1 tsp Eno's fruit salt
Juice from one lemon
1 tbsp oil
Salt to taste

Method

To make the methi muthia, combine the chopped methi leaves, gram flour, wheat flour, turmeric powder, jaggery, asafoetida powder, Eno fruit salt, lemon juice, oil and salt to taste in a small bowl. Add a dash of water to make a firm dough. Divide the dough into 15 small portions. Shape them into tiny rounds like small marbles and keep them aside.

You can choose to steam the muthias in a steamer on high heat for 10 minutes or pan fry in a paniyaram pan. To make them in a paniyaram pan, add a little oil into each cavity of the pan and place it on medium heat.

Place the muthias in the cavities and pan fry them until golden brown and lightly crisp all over. Once done, remove them from the pan and proceed to make the remaining muthias, if any. Keep aside.

To make the Shaak, heat a teaspoon of oil in the pressure cooker on medium heat. Then add the ajwain seeds, mustard seeds and asafoetida. When the seeds splutter, add the ginger and garlic and sauté for a few seconds. Add the chopped tomatoes, turmeric powder, coriander powder, cumin powder, chilli powder, jaggery and salt, and sauté for a few seconds until the masalas come together. We don't have to wait for the tomatoes to become mushy as they will get cooked well in the pressure cooker.

Stir in the brinjal, the cut flat beans and ¼ cup of water. Cover the pressure cooker, place the weight on and cook on high heat for a couple of whistles. Then turn off the heat.

Release the pressure immediately by placing the cooker under cold running water or lifting the weight with a fork. This stops the cooking process of the vegetables and helps the beans and the brinjal retain their vibrant colours.

Open the cooker, and you will notice the semi-gravy-like consistency of the shaak. Check the salt and adjust to taste accordingly.

Add the methi muthia. Turn the heat back on and simmer until the dumplings have absorbed the juices. Once done, turn off the heat and garnish with chopped coriander leaves. Transfer to a serving bowl and serve hot.

~

Bengali Cholar Dal

This wholesome dish is flavoured with a delicate blend of coconut, ghee and whole spices, boosting the natural taste of the chana dal. Did you know that chana dal is high in fibre and has a low glycemic index, which makes it ideal for those with diabetes? In addition, this dal is a brilliant source of zinc, folate, calcium and protein and is low in fat content.

Ingredients

1 cup chana dal, soaked in warm water for 1 hour
½ tsp turmeric powder
2½ cups water
Salt to taste

For the seasoning

2 tsp mustard oil
½ cup dry coconut (kopra), cut into 1-inch pieces
½ tsp cumin seeds
1-inch ginger, finely chopped
2 green chillies, slit
3 dry red chillies
2 cloves
1-inch cinnamon stick
1 bay leaf

Method

In a pressure cooker, add the pre-soaked dal with 2½ cups of water, turmeric powder and salt and cook on high heat for 3 to 4 whistles. Then, turn the heat to low and simmer for 5 minutes and turn off the heat. Allow the pressure to release naturally.

In a saucepan, over medium heat, add a teaspoon of mustard oil. When it is hot, add the dry coconut pieces and fry until they turn golden brown. Once done, transfer the fried coconut pieces to a bowl and keep aside.

In the same pan, heat a teaspoon of mustard oil over medium heat; add cumin seeds, dry red chillies, cloves, bay leaf, cinnamon stick, green chillies and ginger. Sauté until the seeds splutter and the green chilli has a lightly roasted texture.

Stir in the cooked dal and the roasted coconut pieces. Stir well to combine and check the salt and adjust to suit your taste. Bring the dal to a brisk boil for a couple of minutes and turn off the heat. Transfer to a serving bowl and serve hot.

∾

Puran Poli

The first time I had Puran Poli as a part of the main course with a sabzi was at my wedding. I was blown away with the burst of flavours by eating a sweet bread along with a spicy sabzi.

With its perfect blend of flavours from the toor dal to the spices and jaggery, this is simply one of the most delicious recipes you can rustle up in your kitchen. And, trust me, serving it with a valor muthia nu shaak makes it an absolute delicacy.

Ingredients

2 cups whole wheat flour
¼ tsp salt
1 tsp oil
Ghee for cooking

For the filling

1 cup split toor dal, soaked for 20 minutes
1¼ cups water
3/4 cup jaggery, powdered/ crushed
10 saffron strands
1 tsp cardamom powder

½ tsp nutmeg powder

2 tbsp gram flour, or more if required

Method

Drain the water from the soaked dal. In a pressure cooker, add the pre-soaked dal with 1¼ cups of water and cook on high heat for 4 to 5 whistles. After the whistles, turn off the heat. Allow the pressure to release naturally. Once the pressure releases, give the dal a quick mash. The dal should have a thick consistency.

Add the dal and jaggery into a heavy-bottomed pan and place it over medium heat. Keep stirring until the jaggery dissolves completely.

Stir in the saffron, cardamom and nutmeg to the jaggery–dal mix until well combined. Add the gram flour and mix it into the dal mixture and ensure it blends well without any lumps.

Continue stirring the puran poli mix until the dal mix begins to thicken and leaves the sides of the pan. Turn off the heat and allow the puran poli mix to cool completely. Divide the puran mix into 6 portions.

Make the dough for the puran poli. Take a large mixing bowl and add the flour and salt. Combine by adding half a cup of water and then slowly adding more as required. Knead to form a soft and smooth dough. Add a little oil to coat the dough and knead for a couple more minutes until smooth and firm. Divide the dough into 6 portions.

Keep a little flour for dusting on a plate. Roll out the dough into 3-inch diameter circles. Place a portion of the puran poli mix into the centre of the circle. Bring the edges of the circle towards the centre and fold over to cover the entire filling, making sure the edges are sealed well by pinching them together if there is any opening. Flatten the stuffed dough; dust a little flour on your chakla and gently roll out the dough into a 4 to 6-inch-diameter circle, taking care not to put too much pressure as otherwise the puran may spill out of the dough.

Preheat a skillet on medium high heat. Place the rolled puran poli onto the skillet to cook and flip after a minute or so, until you notice light golden brown spots on both sides. At this stage, smear a little ghee on the puran poli and continue to cook to make it crisp and delicious. When you are ready to serve the puran poli, you can smear it with a little more ghee (optional) and serve hot.

MEAL PLAN 4

What's on the Plate?

- Palak Paneer (Cottage Cheese in Spinach Gravy)
- Dal Makhani (Delicately Spiced Black Lentil Gravy)
- Tawa Paratha (Pan-Fried Flatbread; p. 154)
- Lassi (Flavoured Buttermilk; p. 156)
- Lacha Pyaz (Pickled Onions; p. 155)

There are days when I get excited just thinking of making this meal—a classic north Indian meal packed with protein and nutrition—which is also a family favourite. The stars of this culinary combination are palak paneer and dal makhani served with tawa paratha, lacha pyaz and lassi. For rice eaters or for a special weekend lunch, you can also add a Kashmiri pulao to give the meal a royal touch.

Palak Paneer

Palak paneer has been one of my favourite dishes since the time I was a child, and now my children love it as well. Paneer and spinach are protein powerhouses, while spinach is also rich in vitamins and minerals, making this meal plan one of the healthiest in this book.

Ingredients

200 gm paneer, cut into cubes
500 gm spinach leaves, washed and chopped
1 tbsp ghee or butter
2 cloves garlic, finely chopped
1-inch ginger, finely chopped
1 tomato, finely chopped

2 green chillies, slit
1 tsp cumin powder
1 tsp garam masala powder
Salt to taste

For the seasoning

1 tbsp butter
½ tsp cumin seeds
1 bay leaf
1-inch cinnamon stick
2 tbsp fresh cream

Method

Heat the ghee in a pressure cooker over medium heat. Add the ginger, garlic, tomatoes, green chillies, cumin powder and garam masala powder. Sauté for a few seconds, until the tomatoes turn slightly soft.

Add the chopped spinach and the salt and stir. Then, add one tablespoon of water. Cover the pressure cooker and cook the spinach for just one whistle. Then turn off the heat and release the pressure immediately by using a fork and lifting the weight or by placing the cooker under cold running water. After the pressure is released, open the cooker and allow the spinach to cool completely.

Once cooled, pulse the spinach in a blender to make a smooth puree. You can also choose to mash the spinach with a masher; this gives it a chunky texture.

To make the palak paneer, melt the butter in a saucepan on medium heat. Add the cumin seeds, cinnamon stick and bay leaf. Sauté the ingredients for a few seconds. Next, stir in the pureed spinach mix, cream and the diced paneer. Give it a stir, check the salt and adjust according to taste.

Bring the palak paneer to a brisk boil for 3 to 4 minutes and turn off the heat. Transfer to a serving dish and serve hot.

∾

Dal Makhani

A very popular dhaba food from Punjab in which whole black urad dal is simmered with tomatoes and cream along with spices for hours together to attain a creamy and delicious consistency. Over the years, I have modified the recipe to suit new cooking styles. You will simply fall in love with this one-pot dal makhani recipe made using a pressure cooker. The secret to this dish's mind-blowing taste is dried methi leaves and a delicate smoked coal flavour.

Ingredients

    1 cup whole black urad dal, soaked for 8 hours
    1 tsp cumin seeds
    1 tomato, finely chopped
    1-inch ginger, finely chopped
    2 cloves garlic, finely chopped
    2 green chillies, finely chopped
    1 bay leaf, torn
    1-inch cinnamon stick, broken
    ½ tsp turmeric powder
    ½ tsp cumin powder
    ½ tsp garam masala powder
    1 tsp Kashmiri red chilli powder
    ¼ tsp cardamom powder
    2 tbsp ghee
    ¼ cup fresh cream
    1 tsp kasuri methi (fenugreek leaves)
    Salt to taste
    2-inch small charcoal, for smoking

Method

Heat a tablespoon of ghee in the pressure cooker over medium heat. Add the cumin seeds and allow them to splutter. Add the ginger, garlic and green chillies and sauté for a few seconds.

Add the bay leaf, cinnamon stick, tomato, turmeric powder, cumin powder, Kashmiri red chilli powder, garam masala powder and cardamom powder. Sauté on medium heat until the tomato becomes soft.

Add the soaked dal with more water until the dal mix has at least 2 inches of water above it. Add salt to taste and cover the pressure cooker.

Pressure cook the dal for 4 whistles. After that, turn the heat to low and pressure cook for about 35 to 40 minutes on low heat. Then, turn off the heat and allow the pressure to release naturally.

When you open the cooker, the dal should be cooked well and look very mushy and soft. If the dal has become dry, simply add additional water to make it into a more dal-like and soft consistency.

Heat a tablespoon of ghee in a heavy bottomed pan. Add the cumin seeds and allow them to splutter. Add the cooked dal and cream. Turn the heat to low and simmer the dal makhani for another half an hour. While simmering, keep mashing the dal makhani to make it creamy; this will also give the flavours more depth.

Traditionally, Punjabis are known to simmer their dals for more than an hour or two, to get the intense richness and taste from the dal. But make sure that when you simmer the dal it is stirred occasionally, thereby preventing the dal from sticking to the bottom of the pan.

Finally, during the last 10 minutes of the simmering process, add the dried fenugreek leaves into the dal makhani. Stir well and simmer for another 5 minutes. Simultaneously, you may prepare the coal on another burner.

The final step is to smoke the dal makhani. Heat a 2 to 3-inch piece of coal on a flame for about 5 minutes until it has a few red spots on it from the heat.

Place a small steel cup or katori in the centre of the dal makhani pan and immediately place the hot coal inside. Add a few drops of ghee over the coal and you will notice it beginning to smoke. Cover the pan so that the smoke circulates inside and flavours the dal.

After about 30 seconds, open the lid and remove the cup with the piece of coal. You will notice that the coal has added a delicious smoky flavour to the dal makhani. Turn off the heat and transfer the dal to a serving bowl and serve hot.

MEAL PLAN 5

What's on the Plate?

- Nellikai Rasam (Amla Rasam)
- Sorakaya Palya (Spice Bottle Gourd Stir Fry)
- Vazhakkai Poriyal (Raw Banana Roast)
- Steamed Rice
- Curd
- Appalam

When it comes to a comforting south Indian meal, rasam tops the chart, especially when served along with a roasted vegetable like potato or raw banana. In this meal plan, I have combined a tangy nellikai rasam, which is made from gooseberries (also known as amla) with a Tamil Nadu-style vegetable dish of bottle gourd, locally known as soraikkai (it is the name of the gourd). And don't forget to add raw bananas to this meal because they make a perfect side dish which will leave you feeling satiated. Serve this meal for lunch during a hot summer day or even in the evening during monsoons.

Tip: As an alternative for regular rice, you can serve it with cooked foxtail millets or any millet of your choice. It will add more fibre and proteins to your meal.

∾

Nellikai Rasam

Rasam is a delicious comfort food that has a soupy texture, and this recipe is packed with flavours like pepper, coriander and cumin along with a seasoning of garlic and curry leaves. In this recipe, I have made the rasam using whole gooseberries which are naturally enriched with vitamin C. If gooseberries are not available, you can skip them and add cooked pineapple to make the rasam sweet and tangy.

You can cook the peeled and diced pineapple in a pressure cooker along with 1/2 cup of water and a pinch of salt, for 3 to 4 whistles. Once the pressure has released, simmer it with the rasam.

Ingredients

6 whole nellikai (amla/gooseberry)
¼ tsp turmeric powder
Salt to taste

For the rasam

¼ cup toor dal
1 tbsp ghee
½ tsp mustard seeds
¼ tsp asafoetida powder
1 sprig curry leaves
1-inch ginger, finely chopped
4 cloves garlic, crushed
1 green chilli, slit
4 tomatoes, pureed
½ cup tamarind water (15 gm tamarind)
1 tbsp coriander powder
1 tsp cumin powder
½ tsp red chilli powder
1 tsp jaggery
Salt to taste
A handful of coriander leaves, finely chopped

Method

In a pressure cooker, add the whole nellikai with the turmeric powder and salt. Pressure cook on high heat for 5 to 6 whistles. After the whistles, turn off the heat. Allow the pressure to release naturally. Transfer to a bowl and keep aside.

In the same pressure cooker, add the toor dal along with 1 cup of water and cook on high heat for 4 whistles and turn off the heat. Allow the pressure to release naturally. Once done, open the cooker and mash the dal until the texture is smooth.

Heat the ghee in a large saucepan over medium heat; add the mustard seeds and allow them to splutter. Add the asafoetida, ginger, garlic and curry leaves and sauté for a few seconds.

Add the green chilli, tomato puree, tamarind water, cooked nellikai, cooked toor dal, coriander powder, red chilli powder, turmeric powder, cumin powder, salt and jaggery to taste.

Add 1 cup of water and bring the rasam to a brisk boil for about 10 minutes until you notice that it is frothing around the edges. The froth is an indication that the rasam is ready.

Check the taste of the rasam and adjust the salt and spices accordingly. Turn off the heat and transfer the rasam to a serving bowl and serve hot.

Sorakaya Palya

From Karnataka, this classic dish made with bottle gourd is both simple and wholesome. It is made with basic ingredients from the pantry and cooked using a simple one pot technique using a pressure cooker. It even makes a great side dish along with a simple meal of jowar atta phulka and a beetroot raita.

Ingredients

    1 bottle gourd, peeled and diced
    2 tbsp water
    2 tomatoes, finely chopped
    ½ tsp cumin seeds
    ½ tsp turmeric powder
    2 tbsp sambar powder
    1 sprig curry leaves
    Salt to taste
    1 tsp sesame oil, for cooking

A handful of coriander leaves, finely chopped

Method

In a pressure cooker, heat the sesame oil on medium heat. Add the cumin seeds and allow them to splutter. Stir in the curry leaves, chopped tomatoes, turmeric powder and sambar powder. Sauté the tomatoes until they become soft and mushy.

Next, add the diced bottle gourd, salt to taste and 2 tablespoons of water. Cover the pressure cooker and cook for 2 to 3 whistles and turn off the heat.

Allow the pressure to release naturally. Once the pressure releases, open the cooker, give the palya a stir and adjust the salt according to taste.

Finally, stir in the chopped coriander leaves, transfer to a serving bowl and serve hot.

∾

Raw Banana Roast

Also known as vazhakkai poriyal, this classic dish from Tamil Nadu that has a crispy texture and is imbued with the flavours of asafoetida and black pepper, is a perfect summer dish. Raw banana is a fibre-, vitamin- and mineral-rich vegetable, making it diabetic friendly, too.

Ingredients

2 tbsp sesame oil
½ tsp mustard seeds
1 tsp white urad dal (split)
2 sprig curry leaves, roughly chopped
2 raw bananas
½ cup water
1 tsp black pepper powder
½ tsp turmeric powder
1 tsp asafoetida
Salt to taste

Method

Cut the raw bananas into half with the skin on. Place them in a pressure cooker with half a cup of water and pressure cook on high heat for 4 to 5 whistles. Then turn off the heat and allow the pressure to release naturally. Once the pressure releases, peel the skin off. Next, slice or dice the cooked banana into small pieces.

Heat oil in a heavy-bottomed pan over medium heat. Add the mustard seeds, urad dal and curry leaves and allow them to splutter and the dal to turn golden and crisp.

Add the asafoetida, cooked banana, turmeric powder, black pepper powder and salt to taste.

Roast the banana until it is well combined with the spices and transforms into a light, crispy texture. Ensure you are roasting the banana on medium heat. If required, you can add an additional spoon of oil to give it that crispy texture. Then turn off the heat, check the salt and spices, and adjust according to your taste. Transfer to a serving bowl and serve hot.

MEAL PLAN 6

What's on the Plate?

- Jaisalmer ke Chole (Chickpea Masala Curry from Jaisalmer)
- 15-Minute Paneer Masala (15-Minute Spicy Cottage Cheese)
- Sliced Cucumber
- Puri (Fried Flatbread; p. 155)
- Lacha Pyaz (Pickled Onions; p. 155)
- Chaas (Savoury Buttermilk; p. 157)

It's a family tradition that we make puris and chole on Sundays, and each time I make a different type of chole. However, the Jaisalmer ke chole is always a hit. This is a dish packed with flavours, from whole spices to lots of ghee, which a local chef from a desert campsite had shared with me on one of my visits to Jaisalmer. I have paired this chole recipe with a quick 15-minute paneer masala which makes a speedy Sunday lunch if you're not ordering in. I guarantee you will fall in love with this meal.

Remember, when you are making a meal with puris, it is essential to serve sensible portions of 2 puris per person, which will be just enough to make a satisfying meal.

∾

Jaisalmer ke Chole

Cooked in ghee and whole spices, this delectable dish will make your mouth water just looking at it. The chef who shared this recipe with me told me that for the most delicious-tasting chole, it's important to add 250 grams of ghee for every 1 kilogram of chole. No doubt, ghee added that beautiful texture and taste that we as a family relished—we almost finished the chole from the breakfast buffet counter by ourselves. To replicate the dish at home, I have modified the recipe to make it healthier by adding much less ghee and still retaining its lip-smacking flavour.

Ingredients

2 cups kabuli chana, soaked for 8 hours
4 tbsp ghee
2 onions, thinly sliced
4 cloves garlic, finely chopped
2-inch ginger, finely chopped
2-inch cinnamon stick
4 cloves
2 bay leaves, torn
2 brown cardamom (badi elaichi)
2 tomatoes, finely chopped
½ tsp turmeric powder
½ tsp red chilli powder
½ tsp coriander powder

½ tsp garam masala powder
1 tbsp chana masala powder
Salt to taste
A handful of coriander leaves, finely chopped

Method

Pressure cook the soaked kabuli chana with a little salt and enough water such that it is at least 2 inches above the chana, on high heat for 4 whistles. After the whistles, turn the heat to low and simmer for 30 minutes so that the chana is well cooked. Then turn off the heat and allow the pressure to release naturally. The chana should feel so soft that when you press it between your fingers it will easily mash. Keep this cooked chana aside.

Heat the ghee in a large pan over medium heat. Add the onion, ginger and garlic. Sauté until the onions have become soft and lightly brown. Add the whole spices—cinnamon, cloves, badi elaichi, bay leaves—and sauté for a few seconds till you can smell the aromas coming through.

Add the chopped tomatoes, turmeric powder, red chilli powder, garam masala powder, coriander powder and chana masala powder. Sauté until the tomatoes become mushy and soft.

Once the tomatoes turn mushy, add the cooked kabuli chana. Stir well, check the salt and add more if required. Cover the pan and simmer the chole for about 40 minutes so that the flavours seep deeply into the chana. Add a little water to adjust the consistency of the chole gravy.

Once done, turn off the heat and stir in the chopped coriander leaves. Transfer the chole to a serving bowl and serve hot.

∿

15-Minute Paneer Masala

Quick, nutritious and easy, this amazing gravy will be a reason for you to start cooking your meals, as it can't get as simple as this recipe. The paneer is simmered in a honey tomato gravy which is light and nutritious.

Meal Plan 1
- Huli Soppu Saaru
- Badanekayi Palya
- Methi Carrot Jowar Thepla
- Tomato Onion Cucumber Raita
- Rice with Ghee

Meal Plan 2
- Nawabi Kofta Curry
- Rajasthani Kadhi
- Paneer Pulao
- Boondi Raita
- Jowar Atta Roti
- Lacha Pyaz
- Jhat Pat Mirchi

Meal Plan 3

- Valor Muthia Nu Shaak
- Bengali Cholar Dal
- Puran Poli
- Curd

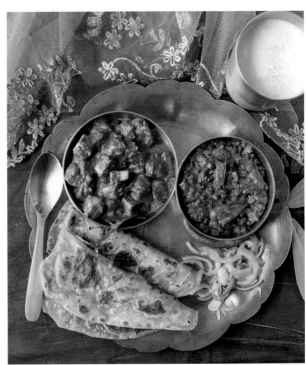

Meal Plan 4

- Palak Paneer
- Dal Makhani
- Tawa Paratha
- Lassi
- Lacha Pyaz

Meal Plan 5
- Nellikai Rasam
- Sorakaya Palya
- Raw Banana Roast
- Steamed Rice
- Curd
- Appalam

Meal Plan 6
- Jaisalmer ke Chole
- 15-minute Paneer Masala
- Sliced Cucumber
- Puri
- Lacha Pyaz
- Chaas

Meal Plan 7

- Rajma Masala
- Gobi Kali Mirch
- Jeera Rice
- Burani Raita
- Lacha Pyaz
- Sliced Cucumbers

Meal Plan 8
- Moong Dal Tadka
- Papad ki Sabzi
- Bhindi Tamatari
- Jowar Atta Roti
- Lacha Pyaz

Meal Plan 9
- Khatta Mag
- Ringna No Olo
- Sev Tameta nu Shaak
- Bajra Na Rotla
- Lacha Pyaz
- Gud
- Chaas

Meal Plan 10
- Vathal Kuzhambu
- Paruppu Usili
- Ragi Atta Roti
- Rice
- Tomato Salad
- Curd
- Appalam

Tip: *while pureeing the tomatoes, add a couple of carrots to puree alongside to boost the nutritional quotient of the gravy. You can serve this dish with tawa paratha for a quick weeknight dinner.*

Ingredients

1 tsp ghee
1 onion, finely chopped
1-inch ginger, finely chopped
4 cloves garlic, finely chopped
6 tomatoes, roughly chopped
2 tbsp fresh cream
½ tsp garam masala powder
½ tsp coriander powder
¼ tsp turmeric powder
1 tsp Kashmiri red chilli powder
1 tbsp honey
250 gm paneer, cut into cubes
1 tbsp kasuri methi (dried fenugreek leaves)
Salt to taste

Method

Add the cut tomatoes to a blender and make a smooth puree and keep aside.

Heat the ghee in a pan over medium heat. Add the onion, ginger and garlic and sauté them until the onions soften and turn lightly golden.

Once golden, add the tomato puree, turmeric powder, red chilli powder, coriander powder, garam masala powder, salt, paneer, honey and cream. Give all the ingredients a quick stir.

Turn the heat to high and allow the paneer masala gravy to come to a brisk boil. Then, cover the pan, turn the heat to low and allow it to simmer for 10 minutes. Once done, give it a stir, check the salt and spices and adjust them according to your taste.

Turn off the heat and transfer the paneer masala into a serving bowl, stir in the kasuri methi and serve hot.

MEAL PLAN 7

What's on the Plate?

- Rajma Masala (Red Kidney Beans Curry)
- Gobi Kali Mirch (Cauliflower Pepper Stir Fry)
- Jeera Rice (Cumin-Flavoured Rice; p. 151)
- Burani Raita (Spiced Garlic Yogurt; p. 148)
- Lacha Pyaz (Pickled Onions; p. 155)
- Sliced Cucumber

A delicately spiced rajma masala, a simple cauliflower stir fry, served with a garlic-flavoured burani raita and jeera rice, this is one of the most comforting meals you can whip up in the comfort of your home. The addition of the easy lacha pyaz with sliced cucumber makes this meal complete. Putting a meal together should be simple, too, so it becomes pleasurable to cook often.

∾

Rajma Masala

This is a classic north Indian dish, and each home has its own unique way of making it. In this recipe, I have shown you how to make rajma masala in the pressure cooker, in a simple and elegant way. The addition of simple spices like cinnamon and cumin powder brings out the delicious taste of rajma.

Ingredients

2 cups rajma, soaked for 8 to 10 hours
1 tsp oil
1 onion, roughly chopped
1-inch ginger, finely chopped

1 bay leaf, torn
1-inch cinnamon stick, broken
2 tomatoes, finely chopped or pureed
¼ tsp turmeric powder
2 tsp cumin powder
1 tsp garam masala powder
½ tsp red chilli powder
Salt to taste
A handful of coriander leaves, finely chopped

Method

In a pressure cooker, heat a teaspoon of oil over medium heat. Add the onion and ginger and sauté for 3 to 4 minutes until the onions soften and turn a light golden.

Stir in the tomatoes, bay leaf, cinnamon stick, turmeric powder, cumin powder, red chilli powder, garam masala powder and salt to taste. Sauté for a couple of minutes until the tomatoes become soft and mushy.

Next, add the soaked rajma along with its water and more, if required. Do ensure the water level is at least 2 inches above the rajma.

Cover the pressure cooker, place the weight on and cook on high heat for 3 to 4 whistles. After the whistles, turn the heat to low and pressure cook for about 30 minutes more. After the half hour is over, turn off the heat and allow the pressure to release naturally. The rajma will continue to cook in the pressure cooker as long as there is pressure inside.

Once the pressure has been released, open the cooker and check the rajma for doneness. If you press the rajma between your fingers, it should easily mash. If you find the rajma is still firm, you will need to pressure-cook it for a little longer. This happens when your rajma bean has aged, and thus, takes a longer time to cook.

Once the rajma masala is cooked, check the salt and spice levels and adjust to suit your taste. Stir in the chopped coriander leaves, transfer to a serving dish and serve hot.

∾

Gobi Kali Mirch

I have grown up eating this cauliflower stir fry—the cauliflower is tossed with pepper and salt and has a light crunch, something we love at home. The simplicity of steamed cauliflower with pepper goes perfectly with dals or other gravy sabzis. Often, I simply eat this with a bowl of curd and make a meal of it.

Ingredients

1 cauliflower, cut into florets
1 tsp cumin seeds
1 tsp black pepper powder
Salt to taste
1 tsp oil

Method

First, steam the cauliflower. You can use a steamer or a pressure cooker to do so. If you are using the steamer, then steam it on high heat for 3 to 4 minutes and then remove from the steamer.

If you use a pressure cooker, place the florets in the pressure cooker, sprinkle some salt, add a tablespoon of water and cover the cooker. Place the weight on and pressure cook for just one whistle.

As soon as you hear the whistle, turn off the heat and release the pressure immediately by placing the cooker under running cold water or using a fork and lifting the weight to release the pressure. The cauliflower, once cooked, will have a firm bite. This is exactly the texture we want for this cauliflower stir fry.

Our next step is to season the cauliflower. Here is where you can experiment with your spices, but I am keeping it simple.

Heat a teaspoon of oil in a kadai over medium heat. Add the cumin seeds and allow them to splutter.

Stir in the black pepper powder and finally, the steamed cauliflower and stir fry until the cauliflower is well coated with the pepper and cumin.

After about a minute, turn off the heat and check the salt and adjust to your taste. Once done, transfer to a bowl and serve hot.

MEAL PLAN 8

What's on the Plate?

- Moong Dal Tadka (Whole Green Moong Dal Seasoned with Ghee)
- Papad ki Sabzi (Spicy Papad Curry)
- Bhindi Tamatari (Okra/Lady's Finger Stir Fry in Spicy Tomato Base)
- Jowar Atta Roti (Sorghum Flatbread; p. 152)
- Lacha Pyaz (Pickled Onions; p. 155)

A fusion meal between the regional cuisines of India is always refreshing and fun. Moong dal tadka paired with a classic Rajasthani papad ki sabzi, succulent bhindi tamatari with fresh-out-of-the-stove jowar atta roti makes this meal wholesome and nutritious. Do be conscious that when you have many dishes on your plate that you serve yourself small portions of each item, and that you eat slowly and mindfully.

Moong Dal Tadka

This is a lip-smacking, dhaba-style dal recipe made with whole green moong dal with a ghee tadka, imbuing it with a delicious aromatic flavour. It is also a lighter version of dal makhani, which makes it perfect for warm summer days. A bonus is that this dish can easily be made in a pressure cooker.

Ingredients

1 cup whole green moong dal, soaked in hot water for at least an hour
1 tsp ghee
1 onion, finely chopped
2-inch ginger, finely chopped

1 tomato, finely chopped
1 green chilli, finely chopped
½ tsp turmeric powder
1 tsp garam masala powder
Salt to taste
2 cups water
A handful of coriander leaves, finely chopped
Juice from one lemon

For the seasoning

1 tbsp ghee
1 tsp cumin seeds
2 dry red chillies

Method

Heat the ghee in a pressure cooker over medium heat. Add onion and ginger and sauté until the onion softens.

Add the tomatoes and green chillies and sauté until the tomatoes turn soft and mushy.

Once done, add the pre-soaked green moong dal, salt, turmeric powder, garam masala and 2 cups of water.

Pressure cook the dal on high heat for 3 to 4 whistles. After the whistles, turn the heat to low and simmer for 10 minutes. Then, turn off the heat and allow the pressure to release naturally.

Once done, give the dal a stir and lightly mash it. Stir in the chopped coriander leaves and the juice from one lemon. Check the salt and adjust it to taste accordingly.

For the tadka, heat ghee in a tadka pan over medium heat. Add the cumin seeds and dry red chillies and roast for a few seconds. Pour the tadka over the dal and give it a stir. Transfer to a serving bowl and serve hot.

Papad ki Sabzi

This Rajasthani dish is made with roasted papad simmered in a tomato and curd gravy and boosted with the flavours of kasuri methi as well as a subtle hit of garlic and green chillies. It is a quick and easy dish, which goes well with phulkas and saag paneer as well.

Ingredients

1 tbsp ghee
½ tsp cumin seeds
¼ tsp asafoetida
1-inch ginger, finely chopped
1 green chilli, finely chopped
3 cloves garlic, finely chopped
1 tbsp kasuri methi
2 tomatoes, pureed
¼ tsp turmeric powder
½ tsp red chilli powder
½ tsp coriander powder
1 tbsp besan (gram flour)
½ cup plain curd, whisked
3 papads
Salt as required
A handful of coriander leaves, finely chopped

Method

Roast the papad over gas flame or in microwave. Break the papad into small quarters and keep aside.

Make a paste of the ginger, garlic and green chillies using a pestle and mortar. Keep aside.

Whisk the gram flour with the curd and keep aside.

In a pan, heat the ghee over medium heat. Add the cumin seeds and allow them to splutter. Add the ginger-garlic-green chilli paste, asafoetida and the kasuri methi. Sauté for a few seconds.

Add the tomato puree, turmeric powder, red chilli powder and coriander powder and give it a brisk boil.

After a minute of boiling, add the whisked curd, roasted papad and salt. Turn the heat to low, then keep stirring until all the ingredients are well combined.

Simmer the mixture for about 5 minutes. You will notice that the curd will begin to curdle a little; this process is completely natural. Allow it to simmer until the papad is well soaked into the curry.

If the curry becomes too thick, add a little water to adjust the consistency to your liking.

Once done, check the taste and adjust the salt and spices accordingly.

Turn off the heat and transfer the papad ki sabzi to a serving bowl and serve immediately.

❧

Bhindi Tamatari

Bhindi—also known as okra or ladies' finger—is a versatile vegetable that blends along with various spices, but it does require a specific cooking technique to ensure that it does not become slimy and sticky post cooking. This recipe of tamatari sabzi is a perfect blend of flavours, from the lightly caramelized onions to the tomato gravy and simple spices. This dish goes well with phulkas and kadhi, too. Bhindi is rich in folic acid and vitamin B6 and is low in calories, making it a good addition to your daily diet as well.

Ingredients

500 gm bhindi, cut into 1½-inch pieces
1 tsp ajwain
2 onions, thinly sliced
3 tomatoes, finely chopped
½ tsp turmeric powder
1½ tsp coriander powder
1 tsp amchur powder

1½ tsp red chilli powder
1 tsp jaggery powder
Salt to taste
Mustard oil or sunflower oil for cooking

Method

In a heavy-bottomed pan, heat 3 tablespoons of oil over low to medium heat. Add the ajwain, then the sliced onions, and sauté them until tender and slightly caramelized.

Once tender, add the bhindi and salt to taste. Cover the pan and keep the lid slightly open. Cook the dish in its steam until the bhindi is tender. Do make sure to keep stirring occasionally. This process takes around 5 to 6 minutes.

It is important to keep the lid slightly open to ensure that part of the moisture being released by the vegetables circulates inside and the remaining escapes; this technique prevents the bhindi from becoming slimy and sticky.

Once the bhindi is tender, add in the tomatoes, turmeric powder, red chilli powder, amchur powder, coriander powder and jaggery.

Continue to cook the dish with the lid slightly open. The tomatoes will release their moisture, and this will cause the bhindi to turn mushy if the lid is closed completely.

In about 10 to 15 minutes, once all the masala has come together, you will have a delicious-tasting bhindi which has a thick tomato-onion masala coated all over it.

Check the salt and spices, and then adjust to taste. Once done, turn off the heat, transfer to a serving bowl and serve hot.

MEAL PLAN 9

What's on the Plate?

- Khatta Mag (Green Moong Dal in Yogurt Curry)
- Ringna No Olo (Spiced Smoked Brinjal)

- Sev Tameta nu Shaak (Fried Gram Flour Vermicelli in Spicy Tomato Curry)
- Bajra Na Rotla (Pearl Millet Flatbread, p. 153)
- Lacha Pyaz (Pickled Onions; p. 155)
- Gud and Chaas (Jaggery and Savoury Buttermilk)

A classic Kathiawadi Gujarati meal with khatta mag, ringna no olo, sev tameta nu shaak and bajra na rotla served with chaas and jaggery. A wholesome meal with plenty of proteins and vegetables packed with minerals, this meal is perfect for winters or during the monsoon season.

Khatta Mag

This dish is similar to kadhi. It is simmered with cooked green moong dal and is packed with the simple flavours of ginger, green chillies and jeera tadka. It is so simple to make and absolutely refreshing to eat that I often consume it as a soupy meal. At home, we often serve it with karela nu shaak and hot phulkas smeared with ghee.

Ingredients

½ cup whole green moong dal, soaked in hot water for an hour
½ cup plain curd
2 tbsp gram flour
¼ tsp turmeric powder
¼ tsp asafoetida
½ tsp mustard seeds
½ tsp cumin seeds
2 sprig curry leaves, roughly torn
1-inch ginger, finely chopped
2 green chillies, slit
1 tsp ghee
Salt to taste
A handful of coriander leaves, finely chopped

Method

In a pressure cooker, cook the soaked green moong with 2 cups of water on high heat for 4 to 5 whistles, and then turn off the heat. Allow the pressure to release naturally.

Whisk the curd, gram flour, turmeric powder, asafoetida, salt and one cup of water until the mixture is smooth with no lumps. Set aside.

In a pan, heat the ghee over medium heat; add the mustard seeds, cumin seeds and curry leaves, and allow them to splutter.

Next, add the green chillies and ginger, and sauté for 30 seconds. To this, add the curd mixture and the cooked green moong dal and stir.

Turn the heat to high and allow the mixture to come to a brisk boil. Keep whisking occasionally to ensure you have a smooth kadhi mixture. After a couple of minutes of boiling briskly, turn the heat to low and simmer for 5 minutes.

Once done, check the salt and adjust to your taste. Turn off the heat, then garnish the dish with chopped coriander leaves. Transfer to a serving bowl and serve hot.

∾

Ringna No Olo

This classic dish from Kathiawad, Gujarat, is very similar to the humble baingan bharta. It is made from roasted brinjals combined with green chillies, ginger and spices, with a dash of curd that brings out its tangy and spicy taste.

Ingredients

2 brinjals (baingan; 500 gm approx.)
½ tsp cumin seeds
2 onions, finely chopped
2-inch ginger, finely chopped
3 green chillies, finely chopped
4 cloves garlic, finely chopped
2 tomatoes, finely chopped
¼ tsp turmeric powder

1 tsp Kashmiri red chilli powder
1 tsp coriander powder
1 tsp garam masala powder
2 bay leaves, torn
1-inch cinnamon stick
2 tbsp ghee
Salt to taste
2 tbsp curd
A handful of coriander leaves, finely chopped

Method

Begin by roasting the brinjal. You can roast the brinjal in two ways—in the oven or on the flame of the stove.

For oven roasting: Preheat the oven to 180°C. Place the brinjal on a baking sheet and place it inside the preheated oven for about 30 minutes or until the brinjal has started to soften and the outer skin is charred. When you test it with a knife, the brinjal should feel tender; if not, continue to bake until you get the required texture.

For flame roasting: Place the brinjal on the stove on the highest flame and, using tongs, turn the brinjal around while it is roasting. Be sure to continuously monitor it. After about 10 minutes, you will notice that the brinjal's skin begins to char and the inside will become tender. To test for doneness, insert a knife into its flesh. It should feel soft. If the flesh is still hard, continue to roast until done.

Allow the brinjal to cool after roasting. Once cool, peel the charred skin and discard it. Using a fork, coarsely mash the pulp. You can also mince it finely using a knife. Set aside.

In a pan, heat the ghee on medium-high heat. Add the cumin seeds and allow them to splutter. Add the ginger, garlic, green chillies, onion, bay leaves and cinnamon stick and sauté them until the onions soften.

Once the onions are soft and golden, add the tomatoes, turmeric powder, chilli powder, coriander powder, garam masala powder and the salt, then sauté until the tomatoes are soft and tender.

Add the roasted brinjal and curd and stir well.

Turn the heat to low and simmer the ringna no olo for about 10 minutes until it is well combined with the tomatoes and spices.

Check the salt and spices and adjust them to suit your taste. Turn off the heat and garnish with freshly chopped coriander leaves. Transfer to a serving bowl and serve hot.

∽

Sev Tameta nu Shaak

This popular Gujarati Kathiawadi dish is often made during festivals, especially during the festival of Paryushan Parva. During this period, people fast for eight days or more, and the few who eat do a partial fast where they abstain from eating all forms of vegetables and only eat grains, fruits and lentils for their meals. Curry leaves, green chillies and coriander leaves are also often avoided during the festival period.

However, we love making this dish at home as it is packed with flavours from green chillies, stewed tomatoes, simple spices and the crunchy sev. It also goes well with thepla and bhakri and makes a simple and scrumptious dinner.

Ingredients

8 tomatoes, halved
1 tbsp ghee
½ tsp mustard seeds
½ tsp cumin seeds
1 sprig curry leaves, finely chopped
2 green chillies, slit
1-inch ginger, finely chopped
½ tsp turmeric powder
1 tsp red chilli powder
1 tbsp jaggery
½ cup sev (fried crispy gram flour vermicelli)
A small bunch of coriander leaves, finely chopped
Salt to taste

Method

Place the halved tomatoes in the pressure cooker with 2 tablespoons of water. Pressure cook the tomatoes for 2 whistles and turn off the heat. Allow the pressure to release naturally.

Next, transfer the tomatoes to a wide plate and allow them to cool. Peel and discard the skin of the tomatoes and finely chop the pulp along with the juices and keep aside.

In a saucepan, heat the ghee on medium heat. Add the mustard seeds, cumin seeds, curry leaves, green chillies and ginger. Sauté for a few seconds and allow the seeds to splutter.

Add the cooked tomatoes, turmeric powder, red chilli powder, jaggery and salt. Sauté until all the ingredients are well combined.

Allow the gravy to come to a brisk boil for 3 to 4 minutes. Then, add the sev with ½ a cup of water, turn the heat to high and bring it to a brisk boil, then turn off the heat.

Check and adjust the salt and spices according to your taste. Once done, stir in the chopped coriander leaves. Transfer to a serving bowl and serve hot.

MEAL PLAN 10

What's on the Plate?

- Vathal Kuzhambu (Sundried Roasted Berries in Tangy Curry)
- Paruppu Usili (Steamed Lentil Crumble with Veggies)
- Ragi Atta Roti (Finger Millet Flat Bread; p. 149)
- Rice
- Tomato Salad
- Curd
- Appalam

Being a Tamilian, I have grown up enjoying many a meal of vathal kuzhambu and paruppu usili served with hot steamed rice topped with ghee. Often, we will end our meal with curd rice and narthangai pickle (sundried citron pickle). With a tangy vathal kuzhambu and paruppu usili served with rice, millet rotis and a few accompaniments, this is the perfect meal for a Sunday brunch.

Vathal Kuzhambu

A sweet, tangy and spicy tamarind curry that uses the delicacy, vathal (dried roasted berries), and roasted pearl onions simmered in sambar powder, vathal kuzhambu makes a delicious accompaniment when served with rice. Manathakkali vathal is a fruit from the black nightshade plant that has many medicinal benefits that aid in digestive and intestinal issues. The dried berries are bitter in taste but, when roasted, they add a wonderful texture to curries.

Ingredients

  2 tbsp manathakkali kai vathal (or sundakkai vathal)
  ½ cup pearl onions, skinned and halved
  1 tbsp sambar powder
  1 tsp jaggery
  1 cup tamarind water (40 gm of tamarind)
  ½ tsp mustard seeds
  ¼ tsp methi seeds (fenugreek seeds)
  1 tbsp sesame (gingelly) oil
  1 sprig curry leaves, torn
  Salt to taste

Method

Heat the oil in a saucepan over medium heat. Add the mustard seeds, fenugreek seeds and the curry leaves and allow them to splutter.

Add the onions and sauté until they are slightly tender and browned. Add in the manathakkali kai vathal or sundakkai vathal and roast until darkened and crispy.

Next, add the tamarind water, ½ cup of water, sambar powder, jaggery and salt.

Turn the heat to high and bring the mixture to a rolling boil for a couple of minutes and then simmer for about 15 minutes.

The kuzhambu should be of pouring consistency and also have a slight pulpiness to it. Adjust the thickness of the gravy by adding a little water, if required. My family likes the gravy slightly on the pulpier side. Many families like to make this recipe by dissolving a teaspoon of rice flour in the gravy as a thickening agent. But I prefer kuzhambu in its original form and like to thicken it naturally over a slow simmer.

Once the kuzhambu has thickened to your satisfaction, taste it and adjust the salt accordingly. Turn off the heat and transfer the vathal kuzhambu to a serving bowl and serve hot.

Paruppu Usili

This steamed lentil crumble with veggies is a popular dish from the Kumbakonam–Thanjavur belt in Tamil Nadu. Paruppu means 'lentil' and usili means 'crumble' in Tamil; in this dish, the steamed and crumbled lentils are tossed with vegetables and seasoned with gingelly oil and the delicate flavours of curry leaves and asafoetida. It goes perfectly with Vathal Kuzhambu, or Mor Kuzhambu, and hot steamed rice topped with ghee.

Ingredients

1 cup split toor dal, soaked in hot water for 1 hour
4 dried red chillies
½ tsp turmeric powder
Salt to taste

For the seasoning

1 cup green beans, finely chopped
1 carrot, finely chopped

1 tbsp gingelly oil

1 tsp mustard seeds

1 tsp white urad dal (split)

2 sprig curry leaves

1½ tsp asafoetida

Method

Drain the excess water from the soaked toor dal and keep aside.

In a mixer grinder, add the toor dal, salt, turmeric powder and dried red chillies and blend to make a coarse mixture. You want the paruppu usili to have a coarse texture when steamed.

Grease the steamer plates or idli plates with oil and spoon the ground paruppu usili mixture on to the steamer plates.

Steam on high heat for 10 minutes. Once steamed, turn off the heat and allow the mixture to cool.

Once cooled, transfer this mixture to a large mixing bowl and crumble the steamed paruppu. This mixture is called the paruppu usili (crumbled dal). Keep this aside.

Next, in a pressure cooker, add the chopped green beans and carrots with 2 tablespoons of water and a dash of salt. Pressure cook on high heat for 2 whistles and turn off the heat. Release the pressure immediately by lifting the weight with a fork so that the beans and carrot retain their bright colours and don't get overcooked.

In a kadai, heat the gingelly oil over medium heat; add the mustard seeds and urad dal and allow the seeds to splutter and the dal to turn golden brown and crisp.

Then, add the asafoetida, curry leaves and the steamed and crumbled paruppu usili to the kadai and mix thoroughly.

Sauté for about 5 minutes until the dish has a perfect crumbly texture. Once you have achieved this texture, stir in the steamed vegetables and turn off the heat.

Check the salt and adjust to taste. Transfer to a serving bowl and serve hot.

MEAL PLAN 11

What's on the Plate?

- Kathirikai Rasavangi (Brinjal Curry in Freshly Ground Spices)
- Beetroot Poriyal (Beetroot Stir Fry—South Indian Style)
- Rice
- Mor Milagai (Sundried Roasted Chillies)
- Chaas
- Appalam

If there is one vegetable I simply love, it is brinjal. Every time I visit my aunt in Chennai, she makes me a delicious rasavangi—a classic dish from Thanjavur. Rasa means 'gravy' and vangi means 'brinjal'. This dish has been adapted from Marathi cuisine which, interestingly, was also a popular cuisine cooked in the Thanjavur kingdom between the seventeenth and nineteenth centuries. I am certain this recipe has gone through its transformation over the years, but the version we make now surely tastes scrumptious.

In this meal plan, I have paired a simple and delectable traditional meal of kathirikai rasavangi, in which brinjal is cooked in freshly ground spices, with beetroot poriyal, and hot steamed rice topped with ghee along with accompaniments like mor milagai, buttermilk and appalam.

Kathirikai Rasavangi

An absolute delicacy in which brinjal is cooked in freshly ground roasted spices and coconut and transformed into a tangy gravy with toor dal. It is often served with hot steamed rice topped with ghee.

Ingredients

1 brinjal, diced
¼ cup split toor dal

½ tsp turmeric powder
1 cup tamarind water (40 gm of tamarind)
1 tsp jaggery, powdered
Salt to taste

For the ground masala

1 tbsp chana dal
1 tbsp coriander seeds
4 dry red chillies
1 tbsp whole black peppercorns
½ cup fresh coconut, grated

For the seasoning

1 tbsp sesame (gingelly) oil
1 tsp mustard seeds
1 sprig curry leaves, torn

Method

In a pressure cooker, add the washed toor dal with ¾ cup of water, turmeric powder and a little salt. Place on high heat and allow it to cook for 2 whistles. Then, turn the heat to low and simmer the dal for around 4 minutes, and turn off the heat. Allow the pressure to release naturally. Once the pressure releases, open the cooker and lightly mash the dal.

Next, dice the brinjal and immerse it in salt water to prevent discolouration.

To roast the masala, heat a small pan on medium heat and dry roast the chana dal until it turns golden brown. Stir in the coriander seeds, red chillies and peppercorns and cook till their aromas are released and the coriander seeds start crackling.

Once roasted, add the grated coconut to the pan and keep stirring until it turns golden brown. Turn off the heat and allow the mixture to cool.

Next, add this mix to the small jar of the mixer grinder with ¼ cup of warm water. Blend to make a smooth mixture. Keep aside.

Heat the oil in a preheated frying pan over medium heat. Add the mustard seeds and allow them to splutter. Add the curry leaves and brinjal, then sprinkle salt and give it a stir. Cover the pan and cook the brinjal until it is roasted and soft.

Once the brinjal has softened, add the tamarind water, turmeric powder, jaggery, cooked dal, coconut mixture and salt to taste. This mixture is the rasavangi.

Simmer the rasavangi for about 5 minutes until the raw smell of tamarind goes away and the curry tastes good.

Check the salt and adjust to taste accordingly. Once done, turn off the heat and transfer to a serving bowl and serve hot.

∾

Beetroot Poriyal

Here is a delicious and healthy preparation of beetroot that is steamed and seasoned with mustard seeds, curry leaves, asafoetida and coconut. Sometimes we add finely chopped onions and roasted peanuts as well to amp up the flavour quotient.

Ingredients

    2 beetroots, finely chopped
    ½ tsp mustard seeds
    ½ tsp cumin seeds
    1 tsp white split urad dal
    1 sprig curry leaves, roughly torn
    ¼ tsp asafoetida
    ¼ tsp turmeric powder
    3 tbsp fresh coconut, grated
    1 tsp sesame oil
    Salt to taste

Method

Place the chopped beetroot in a pressure cooker, sprinkle a little salt over it and add 2 to 3 tablespoons of water. Pressure cook on high heat for 3 whistles and turn off the heat. Allow the pressure to release naturally.

Heat a teaspoon of oil in a heavy-bottomed pan over medium heat. Add the mustard seeds, cumin seeds and urad dal. Allow the seeds to splutter and the urad dal to roast until golden brown and crisp.

Next, stir in the asafoetida, curry leaves, turmeric powder, steamed beetroot and salt and stir fry for about a minute until everything is combined well. Check the salt and adjust to suit your taste.

Finally, garnish with freshly grated coconut and transfer it to a serving bowl and serve hot.

MEAL PLAN 12

What's on the Plate?

- Chawli ki Sabzi (Cowpea Stir Fry)
- Gujarati Dal (Sweet and Spicy Toor Lentils)
- Jowar Atta Roti (Fried Sorghum Flatbread; p. 152)
- Turmeric Pickle (p. 145)
- Curd
- Cucumber Salad

In this simple and wholesome Gujarati meal that is packed with protein and nutrition, the chawli ki sazbi and gujarati dal served with jowar atta roti, turmeric pickle, salad and curd complement each other perfectly. Gujarati cuisine is often a mix of sweet, sour and spicy foods, which lends a very comforting touch to a meal. At home, whenever I make a Gujarati meal, every dish on the table gets wiped clean.

Chawli ki Sabzi

This succulent chawli ki sabzi takes only 15 minutes to make. It is packed with flavours from ajwain and simple spices, which make this sabzi healthy and tasty, too. You can also serve it with kadhi chawal for lunch or dinner.

Ingredients

350 gm green chawli beans, finely chopped
1 tsp mustard oil
1 tsp ajwain
1 tomato, finely chopped
1 tsp red chilli powder
½ tsp turmeric powder
¼ tsp garam masala powder
2 tsp coriander powder
1 tsp amchur powder
1 tbsp jaggery
Salt to taste

Method

In a pressure cooker, add the chopped beans with a dash of salt and 2 tablespoons of water. Pressure cook on high heat for 2 whistles and turn off the heat. Release the pressure immediately to maintain the fresh green colour of the beans.

Heat the oil in a kadai over medium heat; add the ajwain and allow it to splutter. Add the tomato, turmeric powder, red chilli powder, coriander powder and amchur powder, and sauté until the tomatoes become mushy.

Finally, add the cooked green chawli, jaggery, add more salt, if required, and stir well for 3 to 4 minutes.

Once done, taste the sabzi and adjust the seasonings accordingly and transfer to a serving bowl. Serve hot.

❧

Gujarati Dal

This soupy dal has a sweet, mildly spicy and tangy taste. It is full of proteins, flavoured with kokum and a perfect balance of simple everyday spices. If you don't have kokum at home, a squeeze of lemon will boost the flavour of this dal. Serve it with roti-sabzi or make it into a comforting dal-chawal—no matter the combination, this dal is always a winner.

Ingredients

1 cup split toor dal
2 tbsp raw peanuts
2 tbsp jaggery
1 tsp ghee
½ tsp mustard seeds
½ tsp cumin seeds
1 sprig curry leaves, torn
1-inch ginger, finely chopped
1 tomato, finely chopped
1 inch cinnamon stick, broken
1 bay leaf, torn
½ tsp turmeric powder
½ tsp red chilli powder
1 kokum
Juice from one lemon
Salt to taste
A handful of coriander leaves, finely chopped

Method

Pressure cook the toor dal in 2½ cups of water on high heat for about 3 whistles. After the whistles, turn the heat to low and simmer for 3 to 4 minutes and turn off the heat. Allow the pressure to release naturally, as the dal continues to cook while the pressure is still present.

Once the pressure has released, open the cooker and whisk to blend the dal to a smooth texture with no lumps. You can use a hand blender or a potato masher to mash the dal. Transfer the dal to a bowl and keep aside.

Next, add the raw peanuts to the same pressure cooker with ¼ cup water and pressure cook on high heat for 3 whistles, and then turn off the heat. Allow the pressure to release naturally. Keep aside.

Heat the ghee in a saucepan over medium heat; add the mustard and cumin seeds and allow them to splutter.

Add the curry leaves, ginger, cinnamon stick, bay leaf, tomato, turmeric powder, red chilli powder and kokum. Sauté until the tomatoes are soft and mushy. This will take a couple of minutes. You can cover the pan to hasten the cooking process of the tomatoes.

Once the tomatoes are soft, add the whisked toor dal, salt, jaggery, lemon juice and cooked peanuts. Add another ½ to ¾ cup of water, to ensure that the dal has a light, soupy consistency.

Once the dal comes to a brisk boil, turn the heat to low and simmer for about 10 minutes. Check the salt and spices and adjust them to taste accordingly. The dal will taste sweet, spicy and tangy.

Turn off the heat and stir in the chopped coriander leaves. Transfer to a serving bowl and serve hot.

MEAL PLAN 13

What's on the Plate?

- Arachuvitta Sambar (Vegetable Sambar made with Fresh Roasted Sambar Powder)
- Urulai Kizhangu Roast (Spicy Potato Roast)
- Carrot Badam Kheer (Carrot Almond Kheer/Milk Pudding)
- Rice
- Curd
- Appalam

When I was growing up, this meal was one among the many favourite Sunday brunch rituals. I would find my dad in the kitchen, making his favourite potato roast and mom whipping up the remaining dishes. Once the brunch was done, we would sit down to watch *Ramayana* on TV and then take a lovely siesta. On special occasions, there would often be a sweet treat added to this meal. So here is a meal reminiscing old times—fresh arachuvitta sambar served with my dad's spicy potato roast, a carrot badam kheer, rice, curd and Appalam.

Arachuvitta Sambar

This traditional south Indian sambar is made with freshly roasted spices and coconut, which define the burst of flavours when you eat it. This sambar tastes best with seasonal vegetables like radish, pumpkin, drumstick and baby onions—which are a must to give it a fresh flavour.

Ingredients

1 cup split toor dal
¼ tsp turmeric powder
30 gm tamarind, soaked in ½ cup hot water
12 pearl onions (sambar onions), quartered
1 radish, diced
1 carrot, diced
1 tomato, diced
2 drumsticks, cut into 1-inch pieces
1 tsp turmeric powder
Salt to taste

For the roasted sambar powder

2 tbsp coriander seeds
1 tsp chana dal
½ tbsp white urad dal (split)
4 dry red chillies
1 tsp methi seeds
2 tbsp fresh coconut, grated

For the seasoning

1 tsp sesame (gingelly) oil
¼ tsp mustard seeds

¼ tsp asafoetida

2 sprig curry leaves, torn

A handful of coriander leaves, finely chopped

Method

In a pressure cooker, add the washed toor dal with 2 cups of water and turmeric powder. Pressure cook the dal on high heat for 2 whistles. After the whistles, turn the heat to low and simmer for 3 to 4 minutes. Once done, turn off the heat and allow the pressure to release naturally. Once the pressure is released, open the cooker and mash the dal until smooth. Keep aside.

Soak the tamarind in hot water for about 15 minutes. Extract the water from the soaked tamarind pulp by mashing it with your fingers. Do this extraction twice so that you get about 1½ cups of tamarind water. Keep the water aside and discard the pulp.

For the roasted sambar powder, heat a small skillet over low to medium heat. Roast the chana dal and urad dal until the dals have turned brown and lightly crisp. It is important to roast on low to medium heat so that the dals don't brown too fast.

Once the dals are roasted, stir in the coriander seeds, methi seeds and red chillies and roast for about a minute until you can smell the aromas of the spices coming through and the seeds are crackling.

Finally, stir in the grated coconut and roast until the aroma comes through and the coconut begins to change colour. Turn off the heat.

Allow the roasted sambar powder mixture to cool. Once cooled, add the mix to a mixer grinder jar to make a powder. Keep aside.

In a pressure cooker, add the prepared tamarind water, the cut tomato, carrot, radish, drumstick, onions, turmeric powder, salt and the freshly ground sambar powder. Pressure cook on high heat for a couple of whistles and turn off the heat.

Once the pressure is released naturally, add the cooked dal into the tamarind vegetable mixture. Stir well to combine. Check the salt and adjust to suit your taste.

Then, bring the sambar to a brisk boil on high heat for a couple of minutes. The sambar should be of a thick pouring consistency. If it's too thick, adjust the consistency of the sambar by adding a little water and then simmering it for a few more minutes.

While the sambar is simmering, in a small tadka pan, heat the sesame oil over medium heat; add the mustard seeds and curry leaves and allow the mixture to splutter. Finally, add the asafoetida and stir. Turn off the heat.

Stir in the seasoning into the simmering sambar along with the chopped coriander leaves. Turn off the heat and transfer to a serving bowl and serve hot.

∾

Urulai Kizhangu Roast

This classic dish from Tamil Nadu is often served with a sambar and rasam meal. Boiled regular or baby potatoes are roasted with asafoetida, turmeric, chilli powder and salt until the potatoes have a slightly crunchy outer crust. The potato roast makes a great side dish when served with arachuvitta sambar and steamed rice topped with ghee.

Ingredients

300 gm baby potatoes, boiled and peeled
½ tsp asafoetida
¼ tsp mustard seeds
¼ tsp cumin seeds
½ tsp turmeric powder
1½ tsp red chilli powder
4 sprig curry leaves, torn
2 tbsp sesame (gingelly) oil
Salt to taste

Method

Add the baby potatoes into the pressure cooker with ¼ cup of water and pressure cook on high heat for 3 to 4 whistles and turn off the heat.

Allow the pressure to release naturally. Once the pressure is released, open the cooker and allow the potatoes to cool down completely.

Once cool, peel the potatoes and cut them in half if they are too large, and keep aside.

Heat the oil in a kadai over medium heat. Add the mustard seeds, cumin seeds, curry leaves and asafoetida and allow them to splutter.

Add the potatoes, turmeric powder, salt and red chilli powder and mix well until the potatoes are well coated with the ingredients. Cover the pan with a lid and roast the potatoes on low to medium heat, stirring occasionally.

Roast the potatoes until they have a slightly golden brown and crispy outer texture. Remember, potatoes absorb a lot of oil, so adding more oil will give a more roasted feel but be cautious not to add to much.

Once the potatoes are well roasted, check the salt and spice levels and adjust them to suit your taste. Turn off the heat and transfer to a serving dish and serve hot.

ᕬ

Carrot Badam Kheer

My mother often made this wonderful kheer because it killed two birds with one stone—we ate our carrots and had our milk in one nutritious dish! It is extremely simple to make and, with no added sugars, it is perfect as a sweet dish for a festive occasion.

Ingredients

    3 carrots, peeled and grated
    ½ cup whole almonds
    5 dates pitted
    500 ml milk
    A pinch of saffron strands

Method

Soak the almonds in warm water for half an hour. After half an hour, you will notice that the almonds' skin would have turned tender and will easily slip off. Remove the skin from the almonds.

Add the carrots, peeled almonds and dates into a blender. Add a little milk at a time and blend to make a smooth puree. Once the mix is smooth, add the remaining milk and blend again. To adjust the sweetness of the kheer, you can add a little jaggery or sugar to this mix.

Transfer the carrot badam kheer to a heavy-bottomed saucepan and stir in the saffron strands. Turn the heat to medium high and bring it to a brisk boil. Adjust the consistency by adding water or more milk according to your taste.

Turn off the heat and transfer to a serving bowl. Serve hot or chilled.

MEAL PLAN 14

What's on the Plate?

- Pudalangai Thoran (Snake Gourd Stir Fry with Coconut)
- Purple Cabbage Poriyal (Purple Cabbage Stir Fry)
- Nendra Pulissery (Raw Banana Coconut Yogurt Curry)
- Moong Sprout Sundal (Spicy Mung Bean Salad)
- Manga Pachadi (Mango Chutney; p. 150)
- Rice
- Curd

Here is a hearty homestyle south Indian meal packed with flavour and taste. This is a completely refreshing satvik meal with no onion or garlic. You can choose to make one vegetable and serve it with pulissery and sundal or fill your plate with vegetables for a special weekend brunch.

∽

Pudalangai Thoran

Snake gourd is a popular summer vegetable in south India. It is usually sliced and cooked in minimal spices with some grated coconut tossed in. This vegetable is a wonderful source of antioxidants and is perfect for those on a diet because it has very few calories.

Ingredients

2 snake gourd (pudalangai), deseeded and sliced into small pieces
1 tsp coconut oil
½ tsp mustard seeds
2 sprig curry leaves, roughly torn
2 green chillies, finely chopped
¼ tsp turmeric powder
½ cup fresh coconut, grated
Salt to taste

Method

Heat the oil in a heavy-bottomed pan over medium heat. Add the mustard seeds and allow them to splutter. Stir in the green chillies and curry leaves and sauté for a few seconds.

Next, stir in the snake gourd, turmeric powder and salt. Sprinkle a few tablespoons of water into the mixture and cover the pan. Turn the heat to low and cook until the vegetable turns soft. This will take about 6 to 8 minutes.

Once cooked, stir in the grated coconut, check the salt and adjust it according to your taste. Turn off the heat, transfer to a serving bowl and serve hot.

Purple Cabbage Poriyal

This is another classic cabbage dish from Tamil Nadu. This poriyal is made with simple seasonings—mustard seeds, curry leaves, salt and freshly grated coconut—and makes a refreshing side dish for meals. You can use either regular or purple cabbage depending on what's available in season. The purple cabbage adds a nice dash of colour, making your meal rather attractive.

Ingredients

500 gm purple cabbage, roughly chopped or sliced thin
Salt to taste

For the seasoning

1 tsp coconut oil
1 tsp mustard seeds
2 tsp white urad dal
2 sprig curry leaves, finely chopped
¼ tsp asafoetida
2 green chillies, slit
¼ cup fresh coconut, grated

Method

In a pressure cooker, add the purple cabbage and 2 tablespoons of water and pressure cook on high heat for 1 whistle, and then turn off the heat. Release the pressure immediately to avoid overcooking the cabbage.

In a heavy-bottomed pan, heat a teaspoon of oil on medium heat. Add the mustard seeds and urad dal. Allow them to splutter and roast till the urad dal turns golden brown.

Next, add the curry leaves, green chillies, purple cabbage and salt to taste. Sauté for a couple of minutes and turn off the heat.

Once done, stir in the grated coconut. Check the salt and adjust it according to your taste. Serve hot.

❧

Nendra Pulissery

Nendra pazham pulissery gets its fresh and sweet flavours from the Nendra Pazham (Kerala banana), which adds a sweet touch to the coconut curry. The curry gets its refreshing flavours from the freshly ground masalas, the coconut and green chillies. The addition of coconut oil, in turn, heightens the taste of the dish. You can also use ash gourd or yellow pumpkin to make this dish if Kerala banana is not easily available.

Ingredients

1 tsp coconut oil
½ tsp mustard seeds
½ tsp cumin seeds
1 sprig curry leaves, roughly torn
2 nendra pazham banana (ripe), peeled and sliced into rounds
¼ tsp turmeric powder
Salt to taste
1 cup curd

To grind

1 cup fresh coconut
3 green chillies
1 sprig curry leaves
1 tsp cumin seeds
½ cup lukewarm water

Method

In a mixer grinder, add the coconut, green chillies, cumin seeds and curry leaves with ½ cup lukewarm water and blend to make a smooth mixture. Keep aside.

In a heavy-bottomed pan, heat the oil over medium heat. Add the mustard seeds and cumin seeds and allow them to splutter.

Next, add the turmeric powder, the torn curry leaves and the nendra pazham with a dash of salt. Stir fry the nendra pazham until it is soft and cooked through. This will not take more than a couple of minutes. Turn off the heat.

Add the coconut mixture and the curd to the cooked nendra pazham.

When you are ready to serve your meal, bring the nendra pazham pulissery to a brisk boil for a couple of minutes and turn off the heat. Check the salt and adjust it according to taste. Transfer the pulissery to a serving bowl and serve hot.

Moong Sprout Sundal

Sundal is a high protein dish which is an integral part of the festivals of southern India, especially the Navratri season. It is often served as a prasadam in temples as well. Having said that, it makes a great high protein side dish and can even be served as a snack. The combination of the mustard seeds and curry leaf seasoning with chopped green chillies and fresh coconut brings a burst of flavours to the sundal.

Ingredients

1 tsp coconut oil
1 tsp mustard seeds
1 tsp cumin seeds
¼ tsp asafoetida
2 sprig curry leaves, finely chopped
2 green chillies, finely chopped
2 tbsp fresh coconut, grated
1 cup green moong sprouts
1 tbsp lemon juice
A handful of coriander leaves, finely chopped
Salt to taste

Method

Heat the oil in a kadai over medium heat. Add the mustard and cumin seeds and allow them to splutter.

Next, stir in the asafoetida, finely chopped green chillies and curry leaves and sauté for a few seconds.

Stir in the sprouted green moong dal and salt to taste. Sprinkle a couple of tablespoons of water, cover the pan and cook the moong sprouts for about 10 minutes until the moong sprouts are steamed through and cooked. Once done, turn off the heat.

Stir in the grated coconut, lemon juice and coriander leaves. Check the salt and adjust to taste accordingly. Transfer to a serving bowl and serve immediately.

MEAL PLAN 15

What's on the Plate?

- Gujarati Undhiyu (Medley of Mixed Veggies Slow Cooked with Fresh Masala)
- Gujarati Kadhi (Sweet and Spicy Yogurt Curry)
- Khandvi (Gram Flour Pinwheels)
- Shrikhand (Saffron-Flavoured Greek Yogurt)
- Raw Mango Pickle (p. 146)
- Ragi Atta Roti (Finger Millet Flatbread; p. 149)

A Gujarati meal is known for its sweet and spicy food and farsans (salty snacks). A typical meal includes roti, dal or kadhi, rice and shaak, and oftentimes a farsan is added. Farsan is usually eaten as a snack but is also served with meals. Here is a classic meal pairing with rich undhiyu served with a Gujarati kadhi, khandvi and shrikhand, which I have combined with a ragi atta roti that will taste best when it is served hot from the stove. You can serve the meal with phulkas or puris as well and make it extra special.

Gujarati Undhiyu

Undhiyu is a delicious medley of vegetables tossed with methi dumplings, and flavoured with the sweet and spicy taste of coconut, green chillies, coriander and lemon. Traditionally, a few of the vegetables are slit and stuffed with the masala, but this recipe is a modified and easier version which does not require the stuffing process. At home, when undhiyu is made, the methi muthia is the true highlight of the dish and the bowl is always wiped clean at the end of the meal.

Undhiyu is often served with methi thepla, khandvi, puran poli, kadhi, masala chora pulav, paka kela raita and mohanthal for a festive meal.

Undhiyu, though a festive dish, is also made as regular fare in many households. Traditionally, the undhiyu is cooked in an earthen pot and placed underground and slow cooked for hours, bringing out its earthy flavours. However, today, we can make great-tasting undhiyu at home and slow cook it on the stove using a a pressure cooker, just like the way my mother-in-law makes at home.

Ingredients

2 tbsp ghee
1 tbsp ajwain
¼ tsp asafoetida
½ cup flat green beans, cut into ½ inch size pieces
¼ cup sweet potatoes, peeled and diced
¼ cup elephant yam, peeled and diced
¼ cup purple yam, peeled and diced
¼ cup raw banana, peeled and diced
¼ cup baby potatoes, peeled and halved
5 small brinjal, cut lengthwise
Salt to taste

For the undhiyu masala

3 tsp sesame seeds, roasted
3 tsp coriander seeds, roasted
1 cup fresh coconut, grated
½ cup coriander leaves, chopped
4 cloves of garlic
1 inch ginger
2 green chillies
½ tsp turmeric powder
1 tsp red chilli powder
1 tbsp lemon juice
2 tsp sugar
1 tsp salt or to taste

For the methi muthia

  ¼ cup methi leaves, finely chopped
  1 cup gram flour
  ½ tsp turmeric powder
  ½ tsp red chilli powder
  ¼ tsp asafoetida
  ¼ tsp Eno's fruit salt
  2 tsp sugar
  Juice of 1 lemon
  1 tsp oil
  Salt to taste

Method

To make the muthia, combine all the ingredients for the muthia in a small bowl, and add a little water to make a firm dough. Divide the dough into 15 small portions. Shape them into ovals and lightly press them down. You can pan fry using a paniyaram pan or deep fry them in a kadai (see below).

To pan fry in a paniyaram pan

Preheat the pan over medium heat and add a little oil into the cavities of the pan. Place the muthia in the cavities and drizzle a little more oil on top. Flip and turn to cook the muthia all over until golden brown.

To deep fry

Preheat oil in a small kadai over medium high heat. Slide in the muthia and deep fry until golden brown.

To make the undhiyu masala, dry roast the coriander and sesame seeds in a small pan placed over medium heat until they start crackling and the aromas come through. Turn off the heat.

In a blender, add all the ingredients for the undhiyu masala with the roasted coriander and sesame seeds. Add ¼ to ½ cup of water and blend to make a smooth paste. Set aside.

Traditionally, Surti Undhiyu is cooked in an earthen pot placed under the ground with a heat source on the top, and it is slow cooked for a few hours. But I'm using a pressure cooker which is faster and gives a delicious result, too.

Heat two tablespoons of ghee in a pressure cooker over medium heat. Add the ajwain seeds and allow them to splutter.

Add all the cut vegetables and layer them with the coconut mixture. Add ¼ to ½ cup of water and pressure cook for 4 to 5 whistles and turn off the heat. Allow the pressure to release naturally.

Once the pressure is released, add the pan fried muthias. Cover the pan and simmer for another 10 minutes. Add more water, if required. Cook until you notice that all the vegetables and the muthias are well coated with the masala.

Adjust the flavour by adding more salt. Muthias absorb a lot of moisture, so you might need to adjust the consistency of the undhiyu by adding a little water. The final texture to look out for is of well-cooked vegetables in a semi thick gravy with the muthias sticking out to be grabbed. Once done, turn off the heat and transfer to a serving bowl, garnish with coriander leaves and serve hot.

Gujarati Kadhi

The Gujarati kadhi is known for its sweet and spicy taste and soupy texture. It has a delectable blend of flavours from green chillies, ginger, cinnamon and cloves and a ghee tadka. Serve it with a meal which has a dry sabzi or make a comforting meal of this by teaming it with khichdi and papad.

Ingredients

For the kadhi

3 tbsp gram flour
1 cup curd
¼ tsp turmeric powder
2 green chillies, slit
1-inch ginger, finely chopped

3 cups water
Salt to taste

For the tadka

1 tbsp ghee
½ tsp mustard seeds
¼ tsp methi seeds
2-inch cinnamon stick, broken
2 sprig curry leaves

Method

In a saucepan, combine the curd and gram flour and whisk until smooth. Add 3 cups of water and whisk until there are no lumps. This is the base of the kadhi.

Stir in the turmeric powder, green chillies, ginger and salt.

Place the saucepan over medium heat. Keep whisking continuously while you bring the kadhi to a brisk boil.

Turn the heat to low and simmer the kadhi for about 15 minutes. Keep whisking occasionally while the kadhi is simmering; this continuous whisking process will prevent the kadhi from curdling and also give it a smooth texture.

For the tadka, heat ghee in a tadka pan over medium heat; add the mustard seeds and methi seeds and allow them to splutter.

Once the seeds splutter, add the cinnamon sticks and curry leaves and stir fry for a few seconds. Turn off the heat.

Add this tadka to the kadhi and continue to boil it for about 5 minutes on low heat. Check the salt and adjust according to your taste and turn off the heat. Transfer to a serving bowl and serve hot.

Khandvi

If there is a farsan we love at home it is khandvi. Khandvi is a super-soft, melt-in-the-mouth savoury Gujarati snack, where gram flour is combined with curd, ginger and green chillies to make a smooth batter, then slow cooked on low heat and spread on a flat surface and shaped into rolls. The addition of the seasoning makes the rolls taste absolutely divine.

Ingredients

1 cup gram flour
1 cup curd
2 cups water
1 tsp green chilli paste
¼ tsp asafoetida
¼ tsp turmeric powder
1 tsp salt or to taste

For the seasoning

½ tsp mustard seeds
½ tsp cumin seeds
1 tsp sesame seeds
6 curry leaves
2 tbsp fresh coconut, grated
2 tbsp coriander leaves, chopped
2 tbsp oil

Method

To make the khandvi mixture, combine the curd and gram flour in a large bowl; mix well until smooth and till there are no lumps. Whisk in the water, green chilli paste, asafoetida, turmeric powder and salt and ensure it is well combined.

Transfer the khandvi mixture to a non-stick pan. Place this on medium heat, stirring constantly to prevent the formation of lumps. Continue stirring on low heat for around 15 minutes till the mixture thickens.

The khandvi mixture will begin to attain a shine. When this happens, turn off the heat and work as quickly as possible, as the mixture will not spread when it cools down.

Spread the hot khandvi mixture on the working kitchen counter or the back of a plate as thinly as possible with a flat spatula. When you have finished spreading the khandvi batter, allow it to cool a little and settle for about 5 to 8 minutes or more.

Repeat this process and continue to spread the entire mixture before it cools down.

After about 10 minutes, begin rolling the khandvi mixture into a log, starting from the top. Repeat this process for the entire spread-out batter. Once the khandvi rolls have been made, cut the rolls into one-inch size logs. Place the cut khandvi rolls on a serving platter.

For the seasoning, heat the oil in a pan over medium heat. Add the mustard seeds, cumin seeds, sesame seeds and curry leaves and allow them to splutter.

Next, sprinkle the seasoning over the khandvi rolls and garnish with the coriander leaves and grated coconut.

This can be made one day in advance and kept in the refrigerator and warmed up in the microwave before serving.

Shrikhand

Shrikhand is a lip-smacking homemade Greek yogurt (hung curd) pudding that is often flavoured with saffron, cardamom and pistachios and is made during festivals and special occasions. You can also add in seasonal fruits, mangoes and grapes to make it a healthier, refreshing dessert.

Ingredients

    500 gm plain curd
    1 cup sugar, powdered
    1 tsp cardamom powder
    12 saffron strands
    ¼ cup pistachios, finely chopped
    Muslin cloth, to use as a sieve

Method

To make the hung curd for the shrikhand, place the plain curd in a muslin cloth sieve or a fine sieve which has very small holes.

Take a large container (the rim of the sieve should be able to sit on the mouth of the container) and place the sieve with the curd over it.

Next, place this container, along with the curd, in the fridge for 5 to 6 hours or overnight. This step strains all the whey from the curd into the container below, leaving behind a curd that is thick and creamy, popularly called hung curd or Greek yogurt. Also, the curd will not get sour because it is refrigerated.

Next, remove the fully strained hung curd from the fridge and discard the collected whey.

Place the hung curd into a large, clean container. Add the saffron, powdered sugar and cardamom powder into the curd and beat well using a ladle to make a smooth shrikhand.

Finally, stir the pistachios into the shrikhand and refrigerate for a couple of hours and serve chilled.

MEAL PLAN 16

What's on the Plate?

- Oriya Ambila (Sweet and Sour Mixed Vegetable Curry)
- Mixed Dal (High-Protein Mixed Lentil Curry)
- Jowar Atta Roti (Sorghum Flatbread; p. 152)
- Amla Pickle (Gooseberry Pickle; p. 144)
- Tomato Salad
- Curd
- Papad

Oriya meals are simple, wholesome and packed with flavour because of the predominant use of mustard oil and panch phoran (five spice) masala. Here is a simple yet protein-packed Oriya meal which will floor you. Serve it with hot steamed rice or phulkas and accompaniments like an instant amla pickle and a salad to make the meal complete.

You can also replace the rice with cooked foxtail millets which will add a great taste to this meal.

∾

Oriya Ambila

Ambila is a traditional dish from western Orissa, and more specifically popular in the community of people known as kuilta. This dish is a sweet and sour medley of vegetables that gets its sourness from tamarind and that is packed with the flavours from panch phoran masala. Cooking it in mustard oil heightens the flavour of the dish.

Ingredients

1 tsp mustard oil
15 gm tamarind, soaked in water
3 cloves garlic, finely chopped
2 green chillies, finely chopped
2 tomatoes, finely chopped
1 tbsp gram flour
¼ cup curd
1 tsp panch phoran masala
¼ cup yellow pumpkin, diced
¼ cup radish, diced
¼ cup colocasia, diced
¼ cup brinjal, diced
1 carrot, diced
2 bhindi, cut into 1-inch pieces
1 drumstick, cut into 1-inch pieces
½ tsp turmeric powder
½ tsp red chilli powder
Salt to taste

Method

Soak the tamarind in hot water for 15 minutes and extract the tamarind water from the pulp. You will get approximately 1 cup of tamarind water. Keep aside.

In a bowl, add the curd, gram flour and ¼ cup water. Combine well and stir until there are no lumps. Keep aside.

Heat the mustard oil in a pressure cooker over medium heat. Add the garlic and green chillies with the tomatoes. Sauté the tomatoes until they become soft and mushy.

Add the panch phoran masala, turmeric powder and red chilli powder. Sauté this mixture for a few seconds. Add the tamarind water, then stir in the salt and the cut vegetables.

Cover the pressure cooker and cook the vegetables on high heat for 2 to 3 whistles and turn off the heat. Once done, allow the pressure to release naturally.

Once the pressure releases, open the cooker and stir in the curd–gram flour mixture and bring the vegetables to a brisk boil for 3 to 4 minutes until the gram flour is well combined to form a delicious ambila. Check the salt and adjust to suit your taste.

Once done, turn off the heat and transfer the ambila to a serving bowl and serve hot.

Mixed Dal

This mixed dal tadka is a staple in my home. I often make it to give my family that extra-needed protein to complement our vegetarian diet. This version has a perfect blend of lentils, legumes and spices which lends it a rich taste. You can also have this dal as a soup on days when you would like to keep your meals simple yet wholesome.

Ingredients

  ¼ cup toor dal
  2 tbsp chana dal

2 tbsp whole masoor dal
2 tbsp split white urad dal
2 tbsp Kashmiri rajma
2 tbsp kala chana
2 tbsp ghee
1 tsp cumin seeds
1 onion, finely chopped
2-inch ginger, finely chopped
2 green chillies, finely chopped
2-inch cinnamon stick, broken
2 cardamom pods
2 bay leaves, torn
2 tomatoes, finely chopped
½ tsp turmeric powder
½ tsp red chilli powder
½ tsp garam masala powder
Salt to taste
Juice of 1 lemon
A handful of coriander leaves, finely chopped

Method

In a large bowl, soak all the dals in warm water for 6 to 8 hours or overnight. Ensure that they are completely immersed in the water.

Heat the ghee in a pressure cooker over medium heat. Add the cumin seeds, onion, ginger and green chillies and sauté until the onions soften.

Add the bay leaves, cinnamon, cloves and cardamom and sauté for a few seconds until you smell the aromas of the spices coming through. Stir in the tomatoes, turmeric powder, red chilli powder and garam masala powder.

Sauté until the tomatoes turn mushy and soft. Add the salt, soaked dals and enough water such that there is at least 2 inches of water above the dals.

Cover the pressure cooker and cook on high heat for 4 to 5 whistles. After the whistles, turn the heat to low and simmer the dal for at least 30 minutes and turn off the heat.

Allow the pressure to release naturally. Once the pressure has released, give the dal a good stir. Mash it gently to suit a texture of your preference.

Check the salt and adjust to suit your taste. Finally, stir in the lemon juice and coriander leaves and turn off the heat. Transfer the dal to a serving bowl and serve hot.

MEAL PLAN 17

What's on the Plate?

- Aloo Parwal (Spicy Potatoes and Pointed Gourd Stir Fry)
- Niramish Shobji Chapor Jhol (Lentil Patties in a Flavourful Veg Curry)
- Carrot Tadka Raita (Spiced Carrot Curd)
- Instant Raw Mango Pickle (p. 145)
- Jhat Pat Mirchi (p. 158)
- Rice

During my stay in Kolkata, when I worked as a software engineer, I never missed a chance to enjoy an authentic Bengali meal. I learnt a lot from my cook who would whip up delicious vegetarian Bengali delicacies for me. Breakfasts began with rosogolla and kachori aloo, and lunch would be another aloo dish along with rice, and so on. Potatoes form an integral part of a Bengali meal and almost every vegetable is combined with potatoes. Here is a Bengali cuisine-inspired fusion meal which my cook often made for me.

∽

Aloo Parwal

Parwal, also known as potol in Bengali, is a popular vegetable in Bengali and Odiya cuisine. It is nutritious and rich in minerals and vitamins. This combination of potatoes and parwal tossed with simple spices makes it a delectable side dish which you can also serve with phulkas or a simple dal or rasam.

Ingredients

2 tbsp mustard oil
½ tsp mustard seeds
½ tsp cumin seeds
500 gm parwal, peeled and sliced into wedges
3 potatoes, peeled and sliced into wedges
1 tsp turmeric powder
1½ tsp red chilli powder
1 tbsp coriander powder
1 tsp amchur powder
Salt to taste

Method

In this recipe, we will cook the vegetables in two stages.

First, heat a tablespoon of the mustard oil in a heavy-bottomed pan over medium heat. Add in the mustard seeds and allow them to splutter. Then, add the parwal, sprinkle the salt and stir to combine well.

Sprinkle a little water over the parwal, cover the pan and allow the parwal to cook on low to medium heat until it is a little soft and cooked through. In the final stage of the cooking process, add half a teaspoon each of turmeric powder and red chilli powder. Give it a stir. Once done, turn off the heat and keep aside.

Next, cook the potatoes. Heat the remaining tablespoon of oil in a pan over medium heat. Add the cumin seeds and allow them to splutter. Add the potatoes and sprinkle in a little salt, stir to combine and cover the pan. Cook the potato until it has softened inside and has a roasted golden brown colour outside.

Finally, stir in the remaining turmeric powder and red chilli powder, along with the coriander powder and amchur powder, and stir for a couple of minutes.

Stir the cooked parwal into the roasted potatoes and stir fry the mixture until it is well coated with the masala to form a delicious-tasting aloo parwal sabzi. Check the salt and adjust it to suit your taste. Once done, turn off the heat, transfer to a serving bowl and serve hot.

Niramish Shobji Chapor Jhol

The niramish shobji chapor jhol is a high protein delicious Bengali-style vegetable curry flavoured with panch phoran and simmered with lentil patties. Serve it with hot steamed rice and an aloo parwal sabzi for a wholesome meal.

Ingredients

1 tbsp mustard oil
½ tsp mustard seeds
2 bay leaves
2 green chillies, finely chopped
2 potatoes, peeled and diced
4 brinjal, cut into wedges
1 carrot, peeled and diced
½ tsp turmeric powder
1 tbsp panch phoran masala
1 tsp salt
1 tsp jaggery

For the chapor

½ cup split masoor dal
¼ cup split chana dal
2 dry red chillies
1-inch ginger, chopped
¼ tsp turmeric powder
1 tbsp mustard oil
A handful of coriander leaves, finely chopped

Method

Soak the masoor and chana dal for 2 hours. Once soaked, drain the excess water, keeping aside about 2 tablespoons of the water.

Add the soaked dals and the dried red chillies, ginger, turmeric powder and salt to a tall jar of a mixer grinder. Blend to make an almost smooth, thick paste. Try not to add more water as we want this to be a thick batter.

Next, we will shallow fry the dal mixture to make chapors (lentil patties). You can either make small patties or make one large one in the pan by adding all the batter and then cutting it into small irregular pieces.

Heat the mustard oil in a heavy-bottomed skillet over medium heat. When the oil is hot, add the lentil paste and flatten it with your fingers to spread it evenly onto the pan. These chapors need not have any definite shape.

Cover the pan and allow the patties to cook through. When you notice that the top is cooked as it has changed colour, flip it to cook the other side. You will know the chapors are cooked through when you notice light brown spots on both sides and the lentil patties are firm to touch. Once done, remove them from the heat and set aside.

Next, heat the mustard oil in a pressure cooker over medium heat. Add the mustard seeds and allow them to splutter. Then, add the panch phoran masala, green chillies and bay leaves.

Once the spices release their aroma, add all the cut vegetables with a little salt and the turmeric powder and the ½ cup of water. Pressure cook for 3 to 4 whistles and turn off the heat. Allow the pressure to release naturally.

Once the pressure has released, break the chapors into irregular 1 to 1½ inch pieces and add them to the vegetables. Add salt and jaggery to taste and adjust the consistency by adding a little more water. If you like your food spicy, add in more chopped green chillies.

Bring the niramish shobji chapor jhol to a brisk boil for a couple of minutes and turn off the heat. Garnish with coriander leaves, transfer to a serving bowl and serve hot.

ᘓ

Meal Plan 11
- Kathirikai Rasavangi
- Beetroot Poriyal
- Rice
- Mor Milagai
- Chaas
- Appalam

Meal Plan 12
- Chawli ki Sabzi
- Gujarati Dal
- Jowar Atta Phulka
- Turmeric Pickle
- Curd
- Cucumber Salad

Meal Plan 13
- Arachuvitta Sambar
- Urulai Kizhangu Roast
- Carrot Badam Kheer
- Rice
- Curd
- Appalam

Meal Plan 14
- Pudalangai Thoran
- Purple Cabbage Poriyal
- Nedra Pulissery
- Moong Sprout Sundal
- Manga Pachadi
- Rice
- Curd

Meal Plan 15
- Gujarati Undhiyu
- Gujarati Kadhi
- Khandvi
- Shrikhand
- Instant Raw Mango Pickle
- Ragi Atta Roti

Meal Plan 16
- Oriya Ambila
- Mixed Dal Tadka
- Jowar Atta Roti
- Amla Pickle
- Tomato Salad
- Curd
- Papad

Meal Plan 17
- Aloo Parwal
- Niramish Shobji Chapor Jhol
- Carrot Tadka Raita
- Instant Raw Mango Pickle
- Jhat Pat Mirchi
- Rice

Meal Plan 18
- Bendakaya Pulusu
- Pudalangai Poriyal
- Chamadumpa Vepudu
- Moong Sprouts Kosambari
- Rice
- Curd
- Appalam

Meal Plan 19
- Kerala Olan
- Vendakkai Poriyal
- Methi Millet Thepla
- Instant Raw Mango Pickle
- Red Rice
- Appalam

Meal Plan 20
- Bhogichi Bhaji
- Takatla Palak
- Carrot Peanut Salad
- Green Chilli Pickle
- Phulka
- Curd

Carrot Tadka Raita

This raita was my go-to meal when the kids were in school and I wanted to whip up a light meal for myself. The combination of curd with raw carrots and a tadka makes this dish wholesome and filling and makes you feel light yet satiated. You can also serve this raita along with parathas or even as a side dish along with your meals.

Ingredients

2 cups curd
2 carrots, grated
2 sprig coriander leaves, finely chopped
½ tsp cumin powder
Salt to taste

For the tadka

½ tsp oil
½ tsp cumin seeds
1 tsp split white urad dal
1 green chilli, finely chopped
1-inch ginger, finely chopped
1 sprig curry leaves, finely chopped

Method

In a mixing bowl, combine the curd, cumin powder and salt to taste and whisk well until smooth.

Add the coriander leaves and grated carrots to the whisked curd. Mix well to combine and keep it aside.

To make the tadka, heat the oil in a pan on medium heat, add the cumin seeds and the urad dal and sauté until the dal turns golden and crisp. Stir in the green chilli, ginger and curry leaves and saute for a few seconds and turn off the heat.

Pour the tadka over the carrot raita, give it a stir and serve it chilled.

MEAL PLAN 18

What's on the Plate?

- Bendakaya Pulusu (Tangy and Spicy Ladies' Finger/Okra Curry)
- Pudalangai Poriyal (Snake Gourd Stir Fry)
- Chamadumpa Vepudu (Spicy Colocasia Stir Fry)
- Moong Sprouts Kosambari (Lentil Sprout Salad with Coconut Seasoning)
- Rice
- Curd
- Appalam

If you love Andhra food, here is a meal you will cherish. The hot, spicy and tangy bendakaya pulusu, served with two types of vegetables and a wholesome moong sprouts salad makes a comforting meal. For a Sunday brunch, add in a payasam/kheer of your choice and make it an extra special meal.

Bendakaya Pulusu

A lip-smacking Andhra-style dish of ladies' finger, popularly called bendakaya pulusu, this dish gets its tanginess from tamarind and the spices used for its sambar powder. It goes perfectly with rice or cooked foxtail millet topped with ghee.

Ingredients

250 gm ladies' finger (bhindi/okra), cut into 1-inch pieces
½ cup pearl onions, quartered
2 sprig curry leaves, roughly chopped
2 tomatoes, finely chopped
30 gm tamarind, soaked in hot water for 20 minutes

½ tsp mustard seeds
½ tsp cumin seeds
½ tsp methi seeds
¼ tsp turmeric powder
½ tsp red chilli powder
½ tsp sambar powder
1 tbsp jaggery
2 tsp gingelly oil
1 tsp salt or to taste

Method

Extract the pulp from the soaked tamarind and keep aside. You can add water twice to extract the water from the pulp and you will get approximately 1½ cups of tamarind water.

Heat 2 teaspoons of sesame oil in a pressure cooker over medium heat. Add the mustard seeds, cumin seeds and methi seeds and allow them to splutter.

Add in the quartered onions and curry leaves and sauté until the onions turn soft and translucent. Next, add the tomatoes and stir for a minute.

Stir in the cut ladies' finger with the tamarind water, turmeric powder, red chilli powder, jaggery, sambar powder and salt. Add ¼ cup water and pressure cook the bendakaya pulusu for 2 whistles and turn off the heat. Allow the pressure to release naturally.

Taste the bendakaya pulusu, and adjust the salt and seasoning accordingly. Transfer to a serving bowl and serve hot.

∽

Pudalangai Poriyal

A refreshing Andhra-style snake gourd stir fry made with onions, garlic and green chillies. This dish pairs amazingly with rasam and pulusu and hot steamed rice—truly a match made in heaven.

Ingredients

- 2 snake gourds (pudalangai), sliced into small pieces
- ½ tsp mustard seeds
- 1 tsp split urad dal
- ¼ tsp asafoetida
- 1 cup baby onions, finely chopped
- 2 cloves garlic, finely chopped
- 2 green chillies, finely chopped
- 1 sprig curry leaves, roughly chopped
- ¼ tsp turmeric powder
- ¼ cup fresh coconut, grated
- Salt to taste
- 1 tsp of coconut or sunflower oil

Method

In a pressure cooker, add the snake gourd, a little salt and a tablespoon of water. Pressure cook on high heat for 1 whistle and turn off the heat. Release the pressure immediately to prevent the vegetable from getting overcooked.

Heat the oil in a heavy-bottomed pan over medium heat. Add the mustard seeds and urad dal and allow the seeds to splutter and the dal to turn golden brown and crisp.

Add the asafoetida, onion, green chillies and garlic and sauté until the onions soften.

Stir in the turmeric powder and curry leaves and sauté for a few seconds.

Finally, stir in the snake gourd and the freshly grated coconut and sauté for about a minute and turn off the heat. Check the salt and adjust to taste accordingly. Transfer to a serving bowl and serve hot.

Chamadumpa Vepudu

Colocasia is also known as chamadumpa in Andhra cuisine and cheppankizhangu in Tamil. It makes a wonderful dish when you toss it with chilli, salt and asafoetida and cook it to get a roasted texture. Serve it along with a meal of hot rasam, pulusu or sambar with rice and salad, making it a delicious and comforting meal.

Ingredients

500 gm colocasia root (chamadumpa)
2 tbsp oil
½ tsp mustard seeds
1 tsp split urad dal
½ tsp asafoetida
1 sprig curry leaves, roughly chopped
1 tsp turmeric powder
1½ tsp red chilli powder
2 tsp coriander powder
Salt to taste

Method

In a pressure cooker, add the colocasia with ½ cup water. Pressure cook on high heat for 3 to 4 whistles and turn off the heat. Allow the pressure to release naturally.

Next, drain the excess water, peel the skin off the colocasia once cooled, then cut them into thick slices. Keep aside.

Heat oil in a kadai or a heavy-bottomed pan over medium heat. Add the mustard seeds and split urad dal and allow the seeds to splutter and the dal to turn golden brown and crisp.

Stir in the asafoetida and curry leaves and sauté for a few seconds.

Stir in the sliced and cooked colocasia, turmeric powder, red chilli powder, coriander powder and salt. Give it a stir, cover the pan and allow the colocasia to absorb all the flavours and get slow roasted. You can add a tablespoon more oil if you would like it to be on the crisper side.

After 3 to 4 minutes, turn the heat to medium and stir fry till the colocasia is lightly crisp outside. Check the taste and adjust the chilli and salt according to your taste.

Once done, turn off the heat and serve hot.

॰॰

Moong Sprouts Kosambari

Kosambari is a very traditional south Indian salad that is made using lentils and seasoned with mustard seeds, green chillies and coconut. It is often served as a side dish as part of wedding meals and festival meals, but it makes for a high protein salad along with an everyday meal, too. The kosambari can also be eaten as a snack or made as an appetizer for parties.

Ingredients

2 cups whole green moong dal, sprouted
1 carrot, grated
¼ cup fresh coconut, grated
½ cucumber, finely chopped
1 tomato, finely chopped
2 green chillies, finely chopped
Juice of 1 lemon
A handful of coriander leaves, finely chopped
1 tsp salt or to taste

For the seasoning

½ tsp mustard seeds
1 tsp white urad dal
1 sprig curry leaves, finely chopped
1 tsp coconut oil

Method

To steam the green moong sprouts, add it into the pressure cooker along with 2 tablespoons of water. Pressure-cook on high heat for one whistle and turn off the heat. Release the pressure immediately by lifting the weight with a fork. Allow it to cool.

In a mixing bowl, combine the steamed green moong, grated carrot, grated coconut, finely chopped cucumber, tomato, lemon, salt, coriander leaves and green chillies. Adjust the amount of green chillies as per your palate. Mix all the ingredients well.

Heat the oil in a small pan over medium heat. Add the mustard seeds and urad dal and allow the seeds to splutter and the dal to turn golden brown and crisp. Once done, turn off the heat and stir in the curry leaves.

Stir the seasoning into the salad and combine well. Taste the dish and adjust the salt accordingly. Transfer to a serving bowl and serve immediately or chilled.

MEAL PLAN 19

What's on the Plate?

- Kerala Olan (Black-Eyed Bean Coconut Milk Curry with Pumpkin)
- Vendakkai Poriyal (Ladies' Finger/ Okra Stir Fry)
- Methi Millet Thepla (Fenugreek Leaves Flatbread)
- Raw Mango Pickle (p. 146)
- Red Rice
- Appalam

Fusion meals are very common at home and I have always loved to experiment, pairing dishes from various cuisines so that the end result is a wholesome meal with a colourful plate, with flavour as the top priority. Here is a delectable combination—a Kerala stew called olan, served with a Tamil Nadu-style ladies' finger and a Gujarati methi thepla. You will be pleasantly surprised how delicious these dishes taste when paired together.

∽

Kerala Olan

Olan is a traditional stew from Kerala that is packed with the sweet taste of pumpkin, which is simmered with black-eyed beans in a light and delicious coconut milk curry. The addition of green chillies and curry leaves with coconut oil boosts the flavours of this dish.

Ingredients

1 cup ash gourd, peeled and diced
1 cup yellow pumpkin, peeled and diced
½ cup black-eyed beans, soaked for 1 hour
3 green chillies, slit lengthwise
250 ml coconut milk, store bought or homemade
Salt to taste
2 sprig curry leaves
2 tsp coconut oil

Method

In a pressure cooker, add the black-eyed beans along with the soaked water. Add more water such that there is at least 1 inch of water above the beans. Stir in a little salt and cook on high heat for 3 whistles. After the whistles, turn the heat to low and simmer for 10 minutes and turn off the heat. Allow the pressure to release naturally. Transfer to another bowl and keep aside.

In the same pressure cooker, add the ash gourd and yellow pumpkin with a little salt and ¼ cup of water. Cook on high heat for 2 whistles and turn off the heat. Release the pressure immediately by lifting the whistle with a fork or running the pressure cooker under cold water. This prevents the vegetables from getting overcooked.

In a heavy-bottomed saucepan, add the cooked ash gourd and pumpkin, black-eyed beans, coconut milk, curry leaves, green chillies and salt to taste. Stir well to combine.

Simmer the Kerala olan on medium heat for 3 to 4 minutes so that the flavours from the curry leaves and green chillies are well incorporated into the vegetables. Add a little water if you'd like the gravy to be a little thinner, but ensure that it isn't too watery.

In the last minute of the simmering process, stir in the coconut oil and turn off the heat. Cover the pan and allow it to rest for about 5 minutes for the flavours to get infused. This resting process makes the flavours from the curry leaves, green chillies and coconut more prominent. Check the salt and adjust it according to your taste.

Transfer to a serving bowl and serve hot.

Vendakkai Poriyal

Here is a simple stir fry made with ladies' finger tossed in mustard and curry leaves, and seasoned with asafoetida, sambar powder and salt. Sambar powder is a versatile spice mix in south India that is used to make a variety of dishes, from stir-fried vegetables to curries and pulusu. It's the garam masala of south India. In this dish, I have also added roasted peanuts for that extra crunch factor, which brings in a great nutty taste to the poriyal.

Ingredients

500 gm bhindi, cut into rounds
2 tbsp mustard or sunflower oil
1 tsp mustard seeds
2 sprig curry leaves, torn
1 tbsp sambar powder
1 tsp amchur powder
1 tsp jaggery powder
½ cup roasted peanuts, coarsely pounded
Salt to taste

Method

Heat the oil in a heavy-bottomed pan over medium heat. Add the mustard seeds and curry leaves and sauté for a few seconds till the seeds splutter.

Stir in the chopped bhindi and sprinkle a little salt. Cover the pan with the lid slightly open and cook the bhindi until it is soft.

Keep stirring in between to ensure the bhindi gets cooked evenly. Keeping the lid slightly open will allow the steam to circulate inside and also release the excess moisture, preventing the bhindi from becoming slimy and sticky.

The bhindi will take about 15 minutes to cook completely. Once cooked, add the sambar powder, amchur powder, jaggery powder and roasted crushed peanuts. Stir gently to combine and allow the dish to simmer for another 3 to 4 minutes, and then turn off the heat.

Check the salt and spices and adjust them to suit your taste. Transfer to a serving bowl and serve hot.

∽

Methi Millet Thepla

Theplas are a staple of Gujarati cuisine. These super-thin flatbreads are often flavoured with methi leaves. It makes a great snack for your travels and can be had for breakfast with a cup of chai. I have adapted the traditional recipe by adding millets, thus making it more nutritious.

Ingredients

1½ cups whole wheat flour
¼ cup ragi flour
¼ cup jowar flour
½ cup methi leaves, finely chopped
½ tsp turmeric powder
½ tsp red chilli powder
¼ tsp asafoetida
2 tbsp curd
2 tbsp oil
Sunflower oil for cooking the thepla
Salt to taste

Method

In a large bowl, combine the whole wheat flour, ragi flour, jowar flour, turmeric powder, red chilli powder, asafoetida, salt and methi leaves.

Add the curd to the flour mixture and knead into a firm, smooth dough, adding a little water only if required to make it a smooth texture. Finally, add two tablespoons of oil to coat the dough and knead well for 2 to 3 minutes until it is firm and smooth.

Preheat an iron skillet on medium heat.

While your skillet is preheating, divide the thepla dough into equal portions. Roll the thepla portions into balls and flatten them with the palm of your hand.

Dust the thepla dough in wheat flour and roll them out into thin circles to approximately 6 inches diameter. As you roll out the theplas, keep dusting the dough in dry flour to prevent them from sticking. Roll out all the thepla dough as thin as you can.

Turn the heat to high and place the rolled out thepla over the pre-heated skillet. After a few seconds you will notice small air pockets on the thepla's surface. At this point, flip the thepla and, using a flat spatula, smear about ½ a teaspoon of oil over its surface. Press the thepla lightly and keep turning it gently on the pan for a few seconds.

Then, flip the thepla and repeat the process. When you notice brown spots on the thepla, remove it from the heat and place it on a flat plate. The theplas cook fast as they are thin and take less than 30 seconds to cook over high heat.

Repeat the process for the remaining thepla dough. Stack the cooked theplas one over the other. Stacking them helps in preserving moisture and prevents the theplas from drying out, thus maintaining their softness.

Once done, store the theplas in a covered roti box without folding them. Serve with a Kerala olan or a curry of your choice.

Note: Since the theplas are thin and cooked on high heat, they cook very fast. If you find the high heat inconvenient, reduce it to medium. Make sure you have your exhaust fan on or windows open, as cooking on high heat on an iron skillet makes the room smoky.

MEAL PLAN 20

What's on the Plate?

- Bhogichi Bhaji (Marathi Style Mixed Vegetable)
- Takatla Palak (Marathi Style Spinach Curry)
- Carrot Peanut Salad (p. 149)
- Green Chilli Pickle (p. 146)
- Phulka (Whole Wheat Flatbread)
- Curd

I have always been fascinated by Marathi cuisine because of its simplicity and perfect blend of flavours and spices, and often, the addition of peanuts and cashewnuts to complement this blend. Here is a classic Maharashtrian meal of bhogichi bhaji and takatla palak. It is often served along with bhakri, which is a semi-crisp flatbread made from millets. You can also serve this meal with phulkas and hot steamed rice. Add a salad for that extra nutritional punch and a green chilli pickle for a chatpata zing.

∾

Bhogichi Bhaji

Bhogichi bhaji is a Maharashtrian delicacy in which mixed vegetables are simmered and cooked in goda masala—a quintessential Maharashtrian spice mix of aromatic spices blended together to give a subtle sweet and spicy flavour. You can get this masala at a specialty store or online. The dish has a rich yet nutty taste, which goes perfectly with takatla palak and hot steamed rice.

Ingredients

2 carrots, peeled and diced
1 potato, peeled and diced

3 small brinjals (250 gm), stalks removed and diced
¼ cup fresh green peas (or fresh hara chana)
10 avarekai (broad beans), cut into ½-inch pieces
5 ber, washed with stems removed (optional)
1 tsp Maharashtrian goda masala
1 tbsp sunflower or peanut oil
½ tsp cumin seeds
1 tsp mustard seeds
¼ tsp asafoetida
¼ tsp turmeric powder
2 green chillies, finely chopped
Salt to taste
A handful of coriander leaves, finely chopped
Juice of 1 lemon

To be roasted and ground

2 tbsp shelled peanuts
2 tbsp sesame seeds

Method

In a small pan, add the peanuts and roast them over low to medium heat until they turn golden and crisp. Keep aside to cool.

In the same pan, roast the sesame seeds over medium heat until they start to splutter, then turn off the heat and keep aside to cool. Once the peanuts and sesame seeds have cooled, add them to a blender to make a powder. Keep aside.

Heat a tablespoon of oil in a kadai over medium heat. Add the mustard and cumin seeds and allow them to splutter.

Then, add the green chillies, asafoetida, goda masala and turmeric powder. Allow the spices to roast for a few seconds. Be careful not to burn the spices.

Add the diced potatoes, brinjal, carrots and flat beans. Sauté the vegetables and let them blend with the spices and masala. Add salt to taste, sprinkle some water over the vegetables, mix them and cook covered for 10 to 12 minutes or till the vegetables are almost cooked.

Add the fresh green peas and cook covered till all the vegetables are completely cooked through. Add 1 to 2 tablespoons of water, if required, so that the vegetables do not burn at the bottom of the pan. The water creates steam that will help the vegetables cook faster as well.

Once the vegetables are cooked through, add the ber (the optional fruit), sesame and peanut powder and stir well to combine. Cook uncovered for a couple of minutes. Check the salt and spice levels at this stage and adjust them to suit your taste.

Finally, garnish with fresh chopped coriander leaves and lime juice. Transfer to a serving bowl and serve hot.

౼

Takatla Palak

Takatla palak is a classic high protein Maharashtrian dish that has a creamy and delicious gravy made with steamed spinach and peanuts, and flavoured with green chillies, garlic and jaggery, which gives the dish a sweet and spicy taste. You can make a simple meal by serving it along with a bowl of hot steamed rice topped with ghee, and serve it for lunch or dinner.

Ingredients

200 gm spinach leaves, washed and finely chopped
3 tbsp chana dal, soaked in hot water for 15 minutes
¼ cup raw peanuts
½ cup curd
2 tbsp gram flour
1 tsp ghee
½ tsp mustard seeds
½ tsp cumin seeds
3 green chillies, finely chopped
3 cloves garlic, crushed
½ tsp turmeric powder

½ tsp asafoetida
½ tsp jaggery
Salt to taste

Method

In a mixing bowl, whisk together the curd, gram flour and ½ a cup of water. Keep aside.

In a pressure cooker, add the chopped spinach leaves and cook on high heat for one whistle and turn off the heat. Release the pressure immediately by lifting the weight with a fork or placing the cooker under running water to release pressure. This process of releasing the pressure immediately will prevent the spinach from getting overcooked and will help retain its bright colours. Transfer to a bowl and keep aside.

In the same pressure cooker, add the chana dal and raw peanuts with the remaining ½ cup of water and pressure cook for about 3 to 4 whistles and turn off the heat. Allow the pressure to release naturally.

Heat the ghee in a saucepan over medium heat. Add the mustard seeds and cumin seeds and allow them to splutter. Add the garlic, asafoetida, turmeric and chillies and stir for a few seconds.

Stir in the cooked spinach, chana dal, peanuts and curd–gram flour mixture. Add the salt and a little jaggery to taste and bring the takatla palak to a brisk boil until it thickens slightly. Once done, check the salt and seasonings and adjust them to suit your taste.

Turn off the heat, transfer to a serving bowl and serve hot.

MEAL PLAN 21

What's on the Plate?

- Moongphali Mirch ki Sabzi (Peanut Long Chilli Stir Fry)
- Panchmel Dal (High Protein 5 Lentil Stew)
- Palak Paratha (Pan-Fried Spinach Flatbread)

- Lemon Rice
- Tomato Onion Cucumber Raita (Vegetables in Spiced Curd; p. 149)

A colourful and protein-packed fusion meal with lip-smacking regional Indian dishes like palak paratha, chatpata moongphali mirch ki sabzi and Rajasthani panchmel dal served with lemon rice and raita. Alternatively, you can serve the main dishes with a jeera pulao, phulkas and lacha pyaz for lunch or dinner.

Moongphali Mirch ki Sabzi

A simple dish made with whole green chillies, or bajji chilli, which is tossed with masala, a touch of amchur powder for tanginess and some roasted and crushed peanuts for that extra crunch. You can also serve this as a side dish along with plain tawa paratha and kadai paneer.

Ingredients

    10 bajji green chilli
    1 tbsp mustard oil
    ½ tsp ajwain
    2 tbsp gram flour
    ½ tsp red chilli powder
    ¼ tsp turmeric powder
    1 tsp amchur powder
    2 tsp coriander powder
    1 tsp garam masala powder
    1 tsp lemon juice
    ¼ cup roasted peanuts, coarsely pounded
    1 tbsp jaggery
    Salt to taste
    A handful of coriander leaves, finely chopped

Method

Split the chillies in half lengthwise and remove the seeds and cut them into 1½ inch pieces.

Heat the oil in a kadai over medium heat. Add the ajwain and allow it to splutter for a few seconds. Stir in the green chillies and sprinkle a little salt and give it a stir.

Turn the heat to low, cover the pan and simmer for a couple of minutes until the chillies begin to sweat a bit and start releasing moisture.

Next, add the red chilli powder, turmeric powder, amchur powder, garam masala powder, coriander powder, gram flour and salt. Give it a stir.

Cover the pan again and stir the chillies occasionally until they are softened.

When the green chillies are cooked, add the coarsely pounded roasted peanuts, a little jaggery and, optionally, lemon juice to give the sabzi that extra tanginess. Mix well and turn off the heat.

Check and adjust the salt and spices according to your taste. Stir in the chopped coriander leaves, transfer to a serving bowl and serve hot.

∾

Panchmel Dal

Also known as panchkuti, panchmel dal is a traditional Rajasthani dal recipe. It is a staple in almost every household in Rajasthan, often served with dal baati. Panch means 'five' in Hindi; in this recipe, five dals are cooked together, along with simple spices and masala, to create a delicious dish. The addition of the ghee tadka heightens the flavour of this dish.

Ingredients

¼ cup arhar dal
¼ cup whole masoor dal
¼ cup chana dal

¼ cup black urad dal
¼ cup green moong dal
2 tbsp ghee
1 tsp cumin seeds
1 onion, finely chopped
4 cloves garlic, finely chopped
1-inch ginger, finely chopped
2 green chillies, slit vertically
1 bay leaf, torn
1-inch cinnamon stick, broken
1 tomato, finely chopped
½ tsp turmeric powder
½ tsp red chilli powder
¼ tsp asafoetida
Salt as required
Juice of one lemon
A handful of coriander leaves, finely chopped

For the seasoning

1 tbsp ghee
1 tsp cumin seeds
2 dry red chillies, broken

Method

Soak all the dals together in water for about 3 hours.

Heat 2 tablespoons of ghee in a pressure cooker over medium heat. Add the cumin seeds and allow them to splutter.

Add the onion, green chillies, ginger and garlic and sauté until the onion softens.

Add the bay leaf and cinnamon stick and sauté for a few seconds until you can smell the aromas of the spices.

Next, add the tomato, turmeric powder, red chilli powder and asafoetida and sauté for about a minute until the tomatoes have slightly softened.

Then, add the soaked dals, salt to taste and add enough water such that it is at least 2 inches above the dals.

Cover the pressure cooker and cook the panchmel dal for about 3 whistles. After the whistles, turn the heat to low and simmer for 20 minutes and turn off the heat. Allow the pressure to release naturally.

Once the pressure has released, check if the dals are cooked enough. They should mash easily if pressed between your fingers. If they haven't achieved this texture yet, cook them for a while more.

Once done, check the salt and adjust it according to your taste. Stir in the juice from the lemon and the coriander leaves and transfer the Rajasthani panchmel dal to a serving bowl.

Finally, make the tadka. Heat the ghee in a pan over medium heat. Add the cumin seeds and red chillies and allow them to roast for a few seconds. Turn off the heat and add this tadka to the panchmel dal and serve hot.

Palak Paratha

Palak paratha is a high protein Indian flatbread that is nutritious, super easy to make and delicious to eat. The secret ingredient is roasted saunf (fennel seeds). Black pepper also adds to the flavour to the dish.

Tip: When making the dough using spinach, it is important to cook the parathas immediately and not store the dough in the refrigerator as the spinach will release moisture over time, making the dough soggy and hard to roll out later on.

Ingredients

200 gm spinach leaves, washed and finely chopped
2 green chillies, finely chopped
2 cups whole wheat flour
1 tsp fennel seeds, roasted and coarsely pounded
1 tsp turmeric powder
1 tsp cumin powder
1 tsp black pepper powder
Salt to taste
Ghee or oil for cooking

Method

Preheat a small skillet over medium heat; add the fennel seeds and roast until it lightly changes colour and you can smell the aromas coming through. Turn off the heat and allow it to cool. Using a motar and pestle, coarsely pound it. Keep aside.

In a large bowl, combine all the ingredients along with the roasted and pounded fennel seeds and knead the dough, adding a little water at a time to make it firm and smooth. Once the dough has formed well, add one tablespoon of oil to coat the dough and knead again for 2 to 3 minutes until the dough is soft and smooth. Divide the dough into 8 portions.

Preheat an iron skillet on medium heat.

Portion the dough into balls and flatten them with the palm of your hand. Toss them in flour and roll them out into circles of approximately 6 inches diameter. Repeat this process until all the portions are rolled out.

Preheat a skillet on medium high heat. Place one rolled out palak paratha on the skillet. After a few seconds, you will notice air pockets forming on its surface. At this point, turn the heat to medium and flip the palak paratha and smear about half a teaspoon of ghee on and around the paratha. Using a flat spatula, press lightly in a turning motion to cook the paratha.

Flip the paratha and repeat the process. When you notice brown spots on both sides of the paratha and can see that the paratha is slightly crisp, remove it from the heat and place it on a platter. Continue to cook the rest of the rolled-out parathas. Serve hot.

Lemon Rice

If you love lemon rice, then give this recipe a try! All you need is some cooked rice, lemons, ginger, green chillies, salt and turmeric, and you will be on your way to make this super-simple and delicious recipe that you can have any time of the day. It also goes well with various dals and raitas.

Ingredients

2 cups cooked rice, day-old rice preferred
½ tsp mustard seeds
2 tsp white urad dal
¼ cup raw peanuts
1 sprig curry leaves, roughly chopped
1-inch ginger, finely chopped
2 green chillies, finely chopped
1 tsp turmeric powder
Salt to taste
1 tbsp sesame oil
A handful of coriander leaves, finely chopped

Method

Ensure you have some cooked rice ready. It helps using day-old rice as the grains will be well separated.

Keep the remaining ingredients handy as this recipe will be made in a jiffy.

Heat the oil in a heavy-bottomed pan over low-medium heat. Add the mustard seeds, urad dal and peanuts. Allow the seeds to splutter and the dal and peanuts to get roasted well until they turn golden brown. Do this on low to medium heat to ensure that the peanuts are well roasted inside out.

Next, add the curry leaves, ginger, green chillies and turmeric powder and stir for a few seconds.

Add the cooked rice, sprinkle some salt and give it a good stir until all the ingredients are well combined and the rice appears well coated. Turn the heat to low, cover the pan and allow the rice to steam with the seasonings for a couple of minutes.

Next, squeeze in the lemon juice and give the rice a good stir. Check the salt and spice levels and adjust them to suit your taste, then turn off the heat.

Stir in the chopped coriander leaves, transfer to a serving bowl and serve hot.

MEAL PLAN 22

What's on the Plate?

- Paneer in White Gravy (Cottage Cheese in Creamy Cashewnut Gravy)
- Palak Chole (Spinach and Chickpeas Curry)
- Puri (Fried Flatbread)
- Instant Raw Mango Pickle (p. 145)
- Sliced Carrot, Cucumber and Onion

Here's a meal idea that's perfect for a Sunday brunch, when you have guests over, or even on a weekday when you feel like eating something special. This puri–chole plate with the addition of a creamy paneer gravy and a side of salad and achaar is a meal that will keep you satiated for a long time. When serving puris with a meal, ensure you eat mindfully and use small portion sizes and limit to just 2 puris for your meal.

∾

Paneer in White Gravy

Popularly known as Mughlai shahi paneer or nawabi paneer, this paneer recipe simmered in whole spices in a decadent cashew gravy is easier to whip up than it sounds. Apart from being a good fit on this plate with chole puri, you can make a quick weeknight dinner of it by serving it with phulkas and a salad.

Ingredients

¼ cup cashewnuts
¼ cup milk
1 tbsp ghee
2 green chillies, slit
1 bay leaf
1 star anise

1 brown cardamom (badi elaichi)
1-inch cinnamon stick
250 gm paneer, cut into small cubes
1 tsp kasuri methi
½ cup curd
Salt to taste

Method

Add the cashewnuts to the small jar of the mixer grinder, then add the milk and blend together to make a smooth paste. Keep aside.

Heat the ghee in a pan over medium heat; add the green chillies, bay leaf, star anise, badi elaichi and cinnamon stick and sauté them for a few seconds.

Add the kasuri methi, cashew paste, curd, salt and paneer.

Bring the gravy to a brisk boil for a couple of minutes. Once done, check the salt and adjust it according to your taste and turn off the heat.

Transfer to a serving bowl and serve hot.

Palak Chole

This chole recipe is made a lot more nutritious with the addition of palak in the gravy, thus packing it with nutrients such as iron and protein.

Ingredients

1 cup kabuli chana (chickpeas), soaked for 8 hours or overnight
2 cups spinach leaves, roughly chopped
1 tomato, roughly chopped
1 green chilli, finely chopped
2 tbsp ghee
1 inch ginger, finely chopped
1 bay leaf, torn into half
2 brown cardamom (badi elaichi)
1 tsp garam masala powder
1 tsp red chilli powder

1 tsp coriander powder
Salt to taste

Method

In a pressure cooker, add the pre-soaked chickpeas with a little salt and water so that the water level is at least 2 inches above the chickpeas. Pressure cook on high heat for about 4 to 5 whistles. After the whistles, turn the heat to low and simmer for 20 minutes, then turn off the heat. Allow the pressure to release naturally as the chickpeas will continue to cook under the pressure.

Add the tomato and green chilli with 2 to 3 tablespoons of water in a blender and blend to make a puree. Keep aside.

Heat a teaspoon of ghee in a pan over medium heat; add in the chopped spinach and sauté until the spinach is soft and tender. Keep this aside to cool. Once cooled, add the spinach to a blender and make a puree. Keep aside.

Note: We cook the spinach separately from the chickpeas as the cooking times for chickpeas and spinach are very different.

Heat a tablespoon of ghee in a heavy-bottomed pan over medium heat. Once the ghee is heated, add in the bay leaf and cardamom pods and sauté for 1 minute or until the spices release their aroma.

Next, add in the ginger, tomato puree, garam masala, coriander powder and red chilli powder and cook until you see the mixture coming together and thickening a little bit.

Add the cooked chickpeas and simmer the chickpeas in the masala for about 10 to 15 minutes.

Once the masala has coated the chickpeas well, add in the pureed spinach and give it a good stir. Check the salt and spice levels and adjust them to suit your taste.

Gently mash the chickpeas a little bit with the back of the ladle to slightly thicken the gravy if required, and turn off the heat. Transfer to a serving bowl and serve hot.

MEAL PLAN 23

What's on the Plate?

- One-Pot Coconut Milk Vegetable Pulao (Vegetable and Coconut Milk Spiced Rice)
- Gatte Simla Mirch Sabzi (Gram Flour Dumpling and Capsicum Stir Fry)
- Rajasthani Kadhi (Garlic-Flavoured Soupy Yogurt Curry)
- Beetroot Salad
- Jowar Atta Roti (Sorghum Flatbread; p. 152)

A meal which includes two delicious dishes from Rajasthan—a Rajasthani kadhi and sukhe gatte simla mirch ki sabzi—served with a flavour-packed coconut milk pulao and a crunchy and colourful beetroot salad. Add a sooji halwa or a kheer to make a special weekend lunch.

One-Pot Coconut Milk Vegetable Pulao

If there is one go-to pulao you can make often, it is this one, which is packed with flavours from coconut milk and whole spices. Serve along with a sabzi or simply along with a kadhi and papad for a quick weeknight dinner.

Ingredients

    1 cup rice, washed
    120 ml coconut milk
    ½ tsp turmeric powder
    ¼ cup green beans, finely chopped
    1 cup cauliflower florets
    1 carrot, finely chopped
    2 cloves garlic, finely chopped

1-inch ginger, finely chopped
2 green chillies, slit
2 cloves
2 cardamom pods
1-inch cinnamon stick
1 bay leaf
Salt to taste
2 tbsp ghee
¼ cup mint leaves, chopped

Method

Heat the ghee in a large saucepan over medium heat. Add the ginger, garlic and green chillies and sauté them for a few seconds.

Next, add the cloves, cardamom, cinnamon stick and bay leaf and sauté for a few seconds until you can smell the aroma of the spices.

Then, add in the vegetables, rice, turmeric powder, salt and coconut milk. Add a cup of water and stir all the ingredients and cover the saucepan.

Turn the heat to high and allow the pulao mixture to come to a boil. Then, turn the heat to low, cover the pan and simmer the rice until the pulao absorbs all the water.

After about 15 to 20 minutes, once all the water is absorbed, turn off the heat and allow the pulao to rest for at least 10 minutes. This will help the rice become fluffy and remain as separate grains.

Once done, stir in the mint leaves and then give the pulao a gentle stir. Serve hot.

Gatte Simla Mirch Sabzi

Gatte ki sabzi is often made as a gravy dish where gram flour dumplings are simmered in a tangy and spicy gravy. I've added a twist to this popular Rajasthani dish by cooking it as a dry sabzi, and tossing it with capsicum and spices. It goes perfectly well with a kadhi, pulao and salad.

Ingredients

For the gatte

1 cup gram flour
½ tsp ajwain
¼ tsp red chilli powder
2 tbsp curd
1 tbsp oil
Salt to taste

For the sabzi

1 tbsp mustard oil
1 tsp cumin seeds
¼ tsp asafoetida
1 green capsicum, diced small
1 tsp turmeric powder
¼ tsp red chilli powder
2 tsp garam masala powder
1 tsp amchur powder
1 tsp coriander powder
Salt to taste
A handful of coriander leaves, finely chopped

Method

In a large mixing bowl, combine all the ingredients for the gatte. Add a few teaspoons of water at a time and knead well for about 5 minutes to make a very soft melt-in-the-mouth dough. Roll the dough into a long cylinder and cut it into 1-inch discs.

Boil water in a large saucepan. Once the water comes to a rolling boil, add the gatte and boil them until they float to the top. When this happens, boil for another 3 to 4 minutes. Drain the gatte and keep aside.

Next, heat mustard oil in a skillet over medium heat. Add the cumin seeds and asafoetida and allow the seeds to splutter for a few seconds.

Stir in the diced capsicum and sauté until it becomes slightly soft and has a roasted texture.

Turn the heat to low, then add the red chilli powder, turmeric powder, garam masala, coriander powder, amchur powder and salt.

Add the cooked gatte and mix well to combine. Sprinkle a little salt and toss well. Cover the pan and cook for about 5 minutes and turn off the heat. Check the salt and seasonings and adjust them according to your taste. Transfer to a serving bowl, garnish with coriander leaves and serve hot.

∾

Rajasthani Kadhi

A kadhi is a classic curd-based curry which makes a refreshing accompaniment for any meal. The Rajasthani kadhi is a thinner version than the Punjabi kadhi and not as sweet as its Gujarati counterpart. This recipe has a perfect blend of flavours, from the crushed garlic and green chillies to the well-seasoned ghee tadka that heightens the dish's flavour.

Ingredients

For the kadhi

    2 tbsp gram flour
    1 cup curd
    ¼ tsp turmeric powder
    ¼ tsp red chilli powder
    5 cloves garlic, crushed
    2 green chillies, finely chopped
    Salt to taste
    3 cups water

For the tadka

    1 tbsp ghee
    ½ tsp mustard seeds
    ½ tsp methi seeds
    4 cloves
    ¼ tsp asafoetida

2 dry red chillies

1 sprig curry leaves, torn

Method

Make a coarse paste with the garlic and green chillies by crushing them in a mortar and pestle. Keep aside.

In a saucepan, combine the curd and gram flour and whisk until smooth.

Stir in the crushed green chillies and garlic, along with the turmeric powder, red chilli powder and salt. Add 3 cups of water and whisk the kadhi mixture well until smooth.

Place the saucepan on medium heat and bring the kadhi to a boil. Ensure you keep whisking the kadhi continuously. This process of whisking is extremely important to ensure that the kadhi has a smooth texture and the whisking prevents curdling as well.

Continue to whisk and boil the kadhi until you notice that the texture is absolutely smooth. At this stage, turn the heat to low and simmer for another 10 minutes.

While the kadhi is simmering, prepare the tadka.

Heat the ghee in a tadka pan over medium heat. Add the mustard seeds, methi seeds and cloves and allow them to splutter. Then, add the asafoetida, dry red chillies and curry leaves and stir fry for a few seconds. Turn off the heat.

Add this tadka to the simmering kadhi and continue to boil for 4 to 5 minutes. Then, turn off the heat, check the salt and adjust it to suit your taste. Transfer the kadhi to a serving bowl and serve hot.

Beetroot Salad

An Indian-style salad that is packed with flavour as well as nutritious vitamins and minerals and that complements any Indian meal. The tanginess from the lemon juice is well balanced with the sweetness from the beet. Fresh coriander leaves along with green chillies are added to lift the salad's flavour, while peanuts add a nice crunch.

Ingredients

2 raw beetroots, grated
¼ cup roasted peanuts, crushed
2 green chillies, finely chopped
A handful of coriander leaves, finely chopped
Juice from 1 lemon
Salt to taste

Method

In a mixing bowl, add the beetroot, roasted peanuts, green chillies, coriander leaves, lemon juice and salt to taste. Stir well to combine.

Serve as a side dish with your favourite meal or even have it as a snack.

MEAL PLAN 24

What's on the Plate?

- Ragi Mudde (Finger Millet Dumplings)
- Tendli Sukke (Ivy Gourd Stir Fry)
- Ulavacharu (Horse Gram Curry)
- Raw Mango Peanut Salad

This hearty country-style meal is one of my favorites. A power-packed meal that is rich in protein, calcium, iron and other minerals and that has ragi mudde served along with ulavacharu, tendli sukke and a crunchy raw mango and peanut salad. Just a single portion of this meal will make you feel satiated and full for hours together.

Ragi Mudde

Ragi mudde is a staple in Andhra and Karnataka cuisine. It is cooked like a thick porridge, rolled into balls and served with a curry and ghee. An absolutely wholesome dish that is packed with calcium and nutrients.

Ingredients

2½ cups hot water
1 cup ragi flour (finger millet/nagli)
2 tbsp ghee
Salt to taste

Method

Heat 2½ cups of water in a saucepan and add salt to it.

Once the water starts to boil, reduce the heat and add 3 tablespoons of the ragi flour and whisk till there are no lumps and it slowly starts to thicken.

Now, add the remaining ragi flour one spoon at a time and keep stirring so that there are no lumps.

Make sure that the heat is on low and ensure you keep stirring until the mixture thickens completely. Cover the saucepan with a lid and leave the ragi mudde mixture aside to cook for about 5 minutes, until you notice it has thickened.

Once the ragi has thickened, add 2 tablespoons of ghee and keep stirring until the ragi has a shine to it. It takes around 10 minutes to make ragi mudde from 1 cup of ragi flour.

Taste the ragi mudde; it should not feel raw.

To shape the ragi into balls, grease a small high-walled bowl with oil or ghee. Place 2 large tablespoons of ragi mudde into the bowl and start twirling it around till it forms a nice smooth ball.

Once done, the ragi mudde can be served hot.

Tip: *The ragi mudde needs to be shaped into a ball while it is hot. Using a small high-walled bowl helps in shaping the ragi mudde easily.*

∾

Tendli Sukke

Here is a delicious preparation of tendli—also known as ivy gourd/dondakkaya/kovaikkai—made with freshly roasted and ground species, which is definitely a keeper. It goes well along with a meal of rasam, sambar or even phulkas and dal along with a salad and chaas to make a complete meal.

Ingredients

500 gm tendli, cut into angular slices
1 tbsp oil
½ tsp mustard seeds
2 sprig curry leaves
Salt to taste

For the sukka masala

¼ cup fresh coconut, grated
2 tsp coriander seeds
1 tsp white split urad dal
4 dry red chillies
1 tbsp jaggery
15 gm tamarind (deseeded)

Method

First, make the sukka masala. Heat a small skillet on medium-low heat. Add the coriander seeds, white urad dal and red chillies and stir for 4 to 6 minutes until the seeds start spluttering and the dal turns golden brown and crisp.

Next, stir in the coconut and roast for another couple of minutes and turn off the heat and allow the mixture to cool.

Transfer the roasted ingredients and the jaggery and tamarind into a mixer jar and blend to a coarse mixture. Do not add any water to this mixture. Keep this aside.

Next, make the sabzi. Heat the oil in a frying pan over medium heat. Add the mustard seeds and curry leaves and allow them to splutter.

Next, add the sliced tendli, sprinkle a few tablespoons of water and salt over it, then cover the pan and cook for 10 minutes on medium heat.

Open the lid and check if the tendli is cooked completely. It should be soft but still have a slight bite to it.

At this stage, add the freshly ground sukka masala and toss well. Check the salt and adjust it according to your taste. Cover the pan and steam cook the tendli for another 3 to 4 minutes. This will allow the masala to get well absorbed into the vegetable.

Check the salt and spices and adjust them to suit your taste. Once done, transfer the tendli sukke to a serving bowl and serve hot.

∾

Ulavacharu (Horse Gram Curry)

This is a spicy and tangy high protein horse gram curry made with freshly ground coconut masala. It is especially delicious when served with mudde, parotta or even hot steamed rice topped with ghee.

Ingredients

1 cup horse gram dal, soaked in hot water for 2 hours
1 onion, roughly chopped
1 tomato, roughly chopped
1 green chilli, roughly chopped
3 dry red chillies
⅓ cup fresh coconut, grated
A handful of curry leaves
¼ tsp turmeric powder
1 tsp sunflower oil
Salt to taste

For the tadka

1 tsp ghee
½ tsp mustard seeds (rai/ kadugu)
2 sprig curry leaves
½ tsp white urad dal (split)
1 dry red chilli

Method

In a pressure cooker, add the pre-soaked horse gram with 1 cup of water and a pinch of salt. Pressure cook on high heat for 4 to 5 whistles. After the whistles, turn the heat to low and simmer for another 10 minutes and turn off the heat. Allow the pressure to release naturally. Set aside.

In a mixer jar, add the coconut, onion, tomato, curry leaves, red chillies, green chilli, salt, turmeric powder and ½ a cup of water. Grind to form a paste.

Heat oil in a saucepan over medium heat. Add the freshly ground masala for the ulavacharu. Cook this masala for 6 to 8 minutes, stirring constantly.

When you notice that the masala is lightly roasted and the aromas are coming through, add the cooked horse gram along with its water. Add ¼ to ½ cup more water if you feel the curry is too thick. Let the ulavacharu simmer for 5 to 6 minutes so that the flavours get well absorbed and it forms a delicious gravy.

Check the salt and seasonings and adjust them to suit your taste.

While the uluvacharu is simmering, heat the ghee in a small pan over medium heat for the tadka. Add the mustard seeds and urad dal and allow the seeds to splutter and the dal to turn golden brown. Finally, stir in the curry leaves and dry red chilli and roast them for a few seconds, and then pour the tadka over the ulavacharu. Transfer the ulavacharu to a serving bowl and serve hot.

Raw Mango Peanut Salad

A refreshing and nutrient-rich salad made with raw mangoes, tomatoes, carrots and cucumbers with a simple seasoning of salt, cumin powder and chaat masala.

Ingredients

1 raw mango, finely chopped
1 carrot, finely chopped or grated

1 cucumber, finely chopped
1 tomato, finely chopped
¼ cup roasted peanuts
A handful of coriander leaves, finely chopped
A handful of mint leaves, finely chopped
Salt to taste
½ tsp black pepper powder
½ tsp chaat masala powder
½ tsp cumin powder

Method

In a mixing bowl, combine the raw mango, carrot, cucumber, tomato, roasted peanuts, coriander leaves and mint leaves and give them a good mix.

Add the salt, pepper, chaat masala and cumin powder and toss the salad. Taste and adjust the seasonings accordingly. Once it is to your liking, transfer the salad to a serving bowl and serve chilled.

MEAL PLAN 25

What's on the Plate?

- Masoor Dal Tadka (Masala Lentil Curry)
- Bihari Karela Aloo Sabzi (Bihari Bitter Gourd Potato Stir Fry)
- Cabbage Poriyal (Cabbage Stir Fry with Coconut)
- Jowar Atta Roti (Sorghum Flat Bread; p. 152)
- Curd

A truly comforting meal with masoor dal tadka made from whole red lentils served with aloo karela sabzi, cabbage poriyal, roti and dahi. You will love this Bihari version of bitter gourd that is tossed along with roasted potatoes and its combination with whole masoor dal tadka, which makes the meal fibre- and protein-rich. Add a salad of your choice or include a bowl of mixed vegetable raita instead of plain curd to make this meal even more nutritious.

∾

Masoor Dal Tadka

A super simple pressure cooker recipe is perfect for those days when you're tired and want to whip up something delicious and wholesome. Sometimes, I just have a big bowl of this dal and call it a night.

Ingredients

1 cup whole masoor dal, soaked in hot water for 2 hours
1 tbsp ghee
1 onion, finely chopped
1 inch ginger, finely chopped
4 cloves garlic, finely chopped
2 green chillies, finely chopped
2 tomatoes, finely chopped
½ tsp turmeric powder
½ tsp red chilli powder
½ tsp garam masala powder
Salt to taste
A handful of coriander leaves, finely chopped
Juice from one lemon

For the tadka

1 tbsp ghee
1 tsp cumin seeds
¼ tsp asafoetida
¼ tsp red chilli powder

Method

Heat a tablespoon of ghee in a pressure cooker over medium heat. Stir in the ginger, garlic and onion and sauté them until the onions soften a little.

Next, add the chopped tomatoes, turmeric powder, green chillies, red chilli powder and garam masala powder. Stir for a few seconds and add the soaked masoor dal and salt to taste along with 2½ cups of water.

Cover the pressure cooker and cook the dal for 3 to 4 whistles. After the whistles, turn the heat to low and simmer for another 5 minutes, and then turn off the heat. Allow the pressure to release naturally.

Next, open the cooker and stir in the coriander leaves and lemon juice. Check the salt and spices and adjust them to taste accordingly. Transfer the masoor dal to a serving bowl and serve hot.

Lastly, make the tadka. Heat the ghee in a pan over medium heat. Add the cumin seeds, asafoetida and red chilli powder. Stir them for a few seconds, then pour the tadka over the masoor dal and serve hot.

Bihari Karela Aloo Sabzi

You will love this chatpata sabzi of bitter gourd and roasted potatoes flavoured with onion and garlic. You can serve this along with dal tadka and roti or along with kadhi and plain rice for a quick meal.

Ingredients

2 karela (bitter gourd), deseeded and cut into thin strips
3 potatoes, peeled and cut into thick slices
2 tbsp mustard oil
1 tsp cumin seeds
4 cloves garlic, finely chopped
2 onions, thinly sliced
½ tsp turmeric powder
½ tsp garam masala powder
1 tsp coriander powder
1 tsp amchur powder
1 tsp red chilli powder
1 tsp jaggery
Salt to taste

Method

In a pressure cooker, add the karela with a little salt to taste and 2 tablespoons of water. Pressure cook the karela on high heat for 2 whistles and turn off the heat. Release the pressure immediately. Keep this aside.

Heat the oil in a kadai over medium heat. Add the cumin seeds, onion and garlic and sauté them until the onion is soft. Add the sliced potatoes, sprinkle the salt and turmeric powder and cook the potatoes until they are well roasted—they should appear golden brown and have a slightly crisp texture.

You can also cover the pan if you like, to steam cook the potatoes so that they cook faster.

Once the potatoes are roasted, add the cooked karela, red chilli powder, garam masala powder, amchur powder, coriander powder and more salt, if needed. You can also add jaggery at this point if you would like to reduce the natural bitterness of the karela.

Stir well to combine all the ingredients. Stir fry for another 4 to 5 minutes so that the flavours are well absorbed by the vegetables. Finally, check the salt and spices and adjust them to taste accordingly.

Turn off the heat and transfer to a serving bowl and serve hot.

Cabbage Poriyal

This simple preparation of cabbage that is pressure cooked and tossed in a mustard seed and curry leaf tadka makes a perfect and refreshing side dish to any meal. Serve it with a phulka-dal combination or even with a rasam-rice combination; it blends in deliciously.

Ingredients

    500 gm cabbage, thinly sliced
    Salt to taste

For the seasoning

    1 tsp coconut oil
    ½ tsp mustard seeds
    2 tsp white split urad dal
    2 sprig curry leaves, torn
    ¼ tsp asafoetida
    2 green chillies, slit
    ¼ cup fresh coconut, grated

Method

In a pressure cooker, add the sliced cabbage along with 2 tablespoons of water and pressure cook it on high heat for 1 whistle, and then turn off the heat. Release the pressure immediately to avoid overcooking the cabbage.

Heat a teaspoon of oil in a heavy-bottomed pan on medium heat. Add the mustard seeds and urad dal and allow the seeds to splutter and the dal to turn golden brown and crisp.

Next, add the curry leaves, asafoetida, green chillies, cooked cabbage and salt to taste. Sauté for a couple of minutes and turn off the heat.

Once done, add the grated coconut, check the salt and adjust it to suit your taste. Transfer the cabbage to a serving bowl and serve warm.

MEAL PLAN 26

What's on the Plate?

- Murungai Keerai Sambar (Drumstick Leaves Sambar)
- Vazhaithandu Poriyal (Banana Stem Stir Fry)
- Avarakkai Poricha Kootu (Broad Beans Lentil Stew)
- Carrot Peanut Salad (p. 149)
- Rice
- Curd

A delicious and healthy meal which features nutritious drumstick leaves sambar served with steamed rice, banana stem stir fry and a stew made of broad beans. This meal is fully packed with fibre, vitamins, minerals and protein from all the vegetables and dals. You can also add jowar atta roti to this meal.

Murungai Keerai Sambar

Murungai keerai, also known as drumstick leaves, is one of India's best superfoods. It is rich in vitamin C and potassium and chock-full of minerals and antioxidants that boost the immune system and protect against cell damage.[3] When it is added to sambar, it transforms the dish into a homely yet delicious offering.

Ingredients

For the sambar

1 cup split toor dal
45 gm tamarind, soaked in hot water for 10 minutes
1½ cups tamarind water (45 gm of tamarind)
200 gm murungai keerai (drumstick leaves), washed and roughly chopped
1 radish, cut into dices
1 cup pearl onions (sambar onions), quartered
2 tbsp sambar powder
Salt to taste

For the seasoning

1 tsp ghee
½ tsp mustard seeds

---

3   Lakshmipriya Gopalakrishnan, Kruthi Doriya, Devarai Santhosh Kumar, 'Moringa Oleifera: A Review on Nutritive Importance and Its Medicinal Application', *Food Science and Human Wellness* 5, no.? (2016): pp. 49–56. https://www.sciencedirect.com/science/article/pii/S2213453016300362.

½ tsp cumin seeds
½ tsp asafoetida
2 sprig curry leaves, torn

Method

To make the tamarind water, after 10 minutes of soaking, use your fingers to mash the tamarind well into the water until it feels completely soft. This process helps to extract the juice and sourness from the tamarind.

Next, strain the tamarind water into a fresh bowl and squeeze out as much extract from the pulp as possible.

Next we will proceed to the second extraction of the remaining tamarind pulp. Add another 1/2 cup of water and mash the pulp once again to make more tamarind water.

Strain this second extract over the earlier one and keep aside.

In a pressure cooker, add the tamarind water, onions, radish, drumstick leaves, salt and sambar powder. Add 1 cup of water and pressure cook on high heat for 2 whistles and turn off the heat. Release the pressure immediately to prevent the murungai keerai from getting overcooked. Transfer to a saucepan and keep aside.

In the same pressure cooker, add the toor dal with 2½ cups of water and the turmeric powder and pressure cook on high heat for 2 whistles. After the whistles, turn the heat to low and simmer for 4 to 5 minutes and turn off the heat. Allow the pressure to release naturally.

Next, open the pressure cooker and mash the dal well using a potato masher.

Add the cooked dal into the murungai keerai sambar masala and stir well. Check the salt and adjust it accordingly.

Heat the ghee in a tadka pan over medium heat. Add the mustard seeds and cumin seeds and allow them to splutter. Add the asafoetida and curry leaves and turn off the heat.

Pour this seasoning over the murungai keerai sambar and bring it to a brisk boil for a couple of minutes, and then turn off the heat.

Transfer the sambar to a serving bowl and serve hot.

∽

Vazhaithandu Poriyal

Vazhaithandu, which is the banana tree stem, when tossed in simple seasonings, is a humble and tasty high-fibre, mineral-rich dish. The addition of grated coconut combined with pearl onions and green chillies heightens the flavours of this dish. You can also serve this with rasam and hot steamed rice for a comforting meal.

Ingredients

300 gm banana stem, finely diced and soaked in 3 tbsp buttermilk
¼ cup pearl onions (sambar onions), finely chopped
2 green chillies, finely chopped
1 sprig curry leaves, roughly torn
½ tsp turmeric powder
½ tsp mustard seeds
1 tsp split white urad dal
¼ cup fresh coconut, grated
1 tsp coconut oil
Salt to taste

Method

In a pressure cooker, add the chopped banana stem with the 3 tablespoons of buttermilk, salt and turmeric powder and cook on high heat for 2 whistles. Then, turn off the heat and allow the pressure to release naturally.

Heat the oil in a pan over medium heat. Add the mustard seeds and split urad dal and allow the seeds to splutter and the dal to turn golden brown and crisp.

Next, stir in the curry leaves, green chillies and onions and sauté until the onions turn soft and tender.

Stir in the cooked banana stem along with the coconut and stir fry this mixture for a couple of minutes until all the flavours come through. Check the salt and adjust it to suit your taste.

Turn off the heat, transfer to a serving bowl and serve hot.

Tip: While using the banana stem, you need to get to the tender-most part of the stem and use that to chop and make the vegetable. Keep peeling off the outer layer of the stem till you reach the tender part and then use accordingly.

∾

Avarakkai Poricha Kootu

Avarakkai poricha kootu is a comforting, high protein side dish cooked with moong dal and broad beans (avarakkai), tempered with curry leaves, urad dal, mustard seeds and asafoetida, and simmered along with a freshly ground coconut kootu masala. It is a staple south Indian dish that is usually served with rasam or sambar and steamed rice.

Ingredients

200 gm avarekai (broad beans), cut into 1-inch pieces
½ cup split yellow moong dal
¼ tsp turmeric powder
Salt to taste

For the kootu masala

½ cup fresh coconut, in pieces
4 dry red chillies
1 tsp cumin seeds
1 sprig curry leaves
¼ cup warm water

For the seasoning

1 tsp coconut oil
¼ tsp mustard seeds
1 tsp split white urad dal
1 sprig curry leaves

Method

In a pressure cooker, add the chopped avarakkai, a pinch of salt and 2 tablespoons of water and pressure cook on high heat for one whistle.

Once done, turn off the heat and release the pressure immediately. Transfer to a bowl and keep aside.

Using the same pressure cooker, add the split yellow moong dal with 1 cup of water, the turmeric powder and a pinch of salt. Pressure cook on high heat for at least 3 whistles and turn off the heat. Allow the pressure to release naturally.

Once the pressure releases, add the cooked avarakkai to the cooked moong dal and give it a stir.

In a mixer grinder, add the grated coconut, cumin seeds, curry leaves and the red chillies with ¼ cup of warm water to a blender and make a smooth paste.

Add the kootu masala to the avarakkai and the dal mixture. Stir well to combine. Check the salt and adjust it according to your taste.

Heat the oil in a tadka pan over medium heat; add the mustard seeds and split white urad dal and allow the seeds to splutter and for the dal to turn golden brown and crisp. Stir in the curry leaves and turn off the heat.

Next, add this seasoning to the mixed avarakkai kootu and give it a stir.

When you are ready to serve, bring the kootu to a brisk boil. You can adjust the consistency of the avarakkai kootu by adding a little water. Keep in mind that the consistency of the kootu is usually on the thicker side. Transfer the kootu to a serving bowl and serve hot.

MEAL PLAN 27

What's on the Plate?

- Ragi Masala Roti (Finger Millet Masala Flat Bread)
- Keerai Karamani Kuzhambu (Spinach Black-Eyed Beans Curry)
- Cauliflower Carrot Peas Sabzi (Vegetable Stir Fry)
- Beetroot Raita (Flavoured Beetroot Yoghurt; p. 147)

A lip-smacking, wholesome meal that includes a ragi masala roti, served with an earthy beetroot raita, keerai karamani kuzhambu and a cauliflower carrot stir fry. Traditionally, Kuzhambu is had along with hot steamed rice and a poriyal, but oftentimes we serve it along with roti and even dosa or cheelas. Here is one of my favorite versions of ragi roti where I combine the dough with grated carrots, finely chopped onions and greens like coriander and dill leaves, making it a refreshing change from regular ragi atta roti.

∾

Ragi Masala Roti

A tasty, nutrition-rich roti made with ragi flour, grated carrots, onions, dill and coriander leaves. Since ragi is a whole grain, it tends to keep you feeling full for a longer time than processed flours. Thus, a dish like this makes for a satisfying breakfast option, leaving you no room to reach out for unhealthy snacks in your mid-morning hours.

Ingredients

2 cups ragi flour
1 onion, finely chopped
2 green chillies, finely chopped
1 carrot, grated
½ cup dill leaves, finely chopped
¼ cup coriander leaves, finely chopped
½ tsp cumin seeds
Salt to taste
Ghee as required for cooking

Method

In a large mixing bowl, add all the ingredients—ragi flour, onion, green chillies, dill leaves, coriander leaves, carrot, cumin seeds and salt—and mix everything together.

Add warm water, a little at a time, to form a soft dough. Keep kneading for five minutes or till the texture of the dough becomes soft. Once done, cover the dough and keep it aside for 15 minutes.

Divide the dough into lemon-sized portions.

Take a portion and place it in the centre of a wet muslin cloth. Using wet fingers, flatten the ball. Continue pressing the dough until you get a flattened circular shape.

Place the roti on a preheated skillet over medium heat. Cook on one side for a few minutes. Gently release the edges and flip gently with a flat spatula to cook on the other side. Drizzle a little ghee on and around the roti and cook it on both sides until it is lightly browned with golden spots and appears crisp.

Repeat the process with the remaining dough portions and serve hot.

Keerai Karamani Kuzhambu

Keerai karamani kuzhambu is made with the nutritious lobia, also known as black-eyed beans, and palak (spinach) cooked in a spicy, tangy coconut gravy. Make it for a weekday lunch or dinner and you can also serve it with jeera rice.

Ingredients

For the coconut masala

    1 tbsp coriander seeds
    4 dried red chillies
    ½ tsp cumin seeds
    ½ tsp methi seeds
    1 tsp black peppercorns
    ½ cup fresh coconut
    30 gm tamarind, soaked in water

For the curry

    1 cup black-eyed beans, soaked for 2 hours

¼ tsp turmeric powder

1 tsp coconut oil

¼ cup pearl onions, quartered

Salt to taste

100 gm spinach leaves, washed and roughly chopped

1 tsp coconut oil

For the tadka

1 tsp coconut oil

½ tsp mustard seeds

2 dry red chillies, broken in half

2 sprig curry leaves, torn

2 cloves garlic, crushed

Method

In a pressure cooker, add the black-eyed beans with 2 cups of water, salt and turmeric powder. Pressure cook on high heat for 3 whistles. After the whistles, turn the heat to low and simmer for 5 minutes and turn off the heat. Allow the pressure to release naturally. Keep aside.

Heat a pan over medium heat. Add the coriander seeds, cumin seeds, methi seeds, red chillies and black peppercorns and roast in a pan till the seeds start spluttering and you can smell the aroma of the spices.

Next, add the coconut and roast for about 30 seconds, and then turn off the heat. Allow the masala mixture to cool a bit.

Once cooled, add the masala to a mixer grinder, along with the soaked tamarind and ½ a cup of warm water, and blend to make a smooth paste. Keep aside.

Heat the coconut oil in a saucepan over medium heat. Add the onion and sauté until it softens and turns slightly brown. Stir in the curry leaves and sauté for a few more seconds.

Add the coconut masala and the cooked black-eyed beans and salt to taste. Add a little water and bring the curry to a brisk boil for 3 to 4 minutes. Once done, stir in the chopped spinach and allow it to soften; it will take just a few minutes. Check the salt and adjust it to taste accordingly.

Finally, for the tadka, heat the coconut oil in a pan over medium heat. Add the mustard seeds, curry leaves, red chillies and garlic. Allow the mustard seeds to splutter and the garlic to turn golden brown, and then turn off the heat.

Transfer the curry to a serving bowl and pour the tadka over the curry. Serve hot.

∽

Cauliflower Carrot Peas Sabzi

A simple stir fry flavoured with whole spices, ajwain, black pepper and salt. It makes for a refreshing dish that you can serve along with a dal tadka and rice for a quick, simple meal.

Ingredients

  1 tsp coconut oil
  ½ tsp ajwain
  ½ tsp turmeric powder
  2 carrots, cut into ½ inch sticks
  2 cups cauliflower, cut into florets
  1 cup green peas
  1 tsp black pepper powder
  Salt to taste

Method

Heat the coconut oil in a pan over medium heat. Add the ajwain seeds and allow them to splutter.

Add the turmeric powder and give it a stir. Add in the carrots, cauliflower florets and green peas. Season with salt and sprinkle some water and stir to mix well.

Cover and cook the vegetables on low heat until the cauliflower and carrots are not only well cooked, but also have a firm bite.

Finally, stir in the black pepper powder and toss well to combine.

Once done, taste the vegetables and adjust the salt accordingly. Transfer to a serving bowl and serve hot.

Meal Plan 21
- Moongphali Mirch ki Sabzi
- Panchmel Dal
- Palak Paratha
- Lemon Rice
- Tomato Onion Cucumber Raita

Meal Plan 22
- Paneer in White Gravy
- Palak Chole
- Puri
- Instant Raw Mango Pickle
- Salad

Meal Plan 23
- One-Pot Coconut Milk Veg Pulao
- Gatte Simla Mirch Sabzi
- Rajasthani Kadhi
- Beetroot Salad
- Jowar Atta Roti

Meal Plan 24
- Ragi Mudde
- Tendli Sukke
- Ulavacharu
- Raw Mango Peanut Salad

Meal Plan 25
- Masoor Dal Tadka
- Bihari Karela Aloo Sabzi
- Cabbage Poriyal
- Jowar Atta Roti
- Curd

Meal Plan 26
- Drumstick-Leaves Sambar
- Banana Stem Poriyal (Vazhaithandu)
- Avarakkai Poricha Kootu
- Carrot Peanut Salad
- Rice
- Curd

Meal Plan 27
- Ragi Masala Roti
- Keerai Karamani Kuzhambu
- Cauliflower Carrot Peas Sabzi
- Beetroot Raita

Meal Plan 28
- Palak Kadhi Pakora
- Bharva Karela Masala
- Kala Chana Salad
- Ragi Atta Roti
- Cut Cucumber
- Curd

Meal Plan 29
- Hariyali Gobi
- Methi Kadhi
- Vegetable Tehri
- Rajma Salad
- Jowar Atta Roti
- Aam Ras

Meal Plan 30
- Cabbage Kootu
- Vazhaipoo Poriyal
- Kathirikai Poondu Pirattal
- Tomato Garlic Rasam
- Paruppu Payasam
- Appalam
- Curd
- Rice

MEAL PLAN 28

What's on the Plate?

- Palak Kadhi Pakora (Spinach Dumplings in Yogurt Curry)
- Bharwa Karela Masala (Stuffed Bitter Gourd Masala)
- Kala Chana Salad (Black Chickpea Salad)
- Ragi Atta Roti (Finger Millet Flatbread; p. 149)
- Cut Cucumber Salad
- Curd

Here's a wholesome meal of palak kadhi pakora served with bharwa karela makhani, a high protein kala chana salad and a mineral-rich ragi atta roti. You can substitute the roti with jeera pulao if you prefer rice, and end the meal with chaas.

Palak Kadhi Pakora

A delicious north Indian kadhi recipe in which spinach and onion pakoras are simmered in a spicy curd gravy. To make it a healthier option, I've made the pakoras healthier by pan-frying it in a paniyaram pan with very little oil.

Ingredients

For the palak pakora

½ cup gram flour
1 cup spinach, finely chopped
1 onion, finely chopped
½ tsp red chilli powder
½ tsp turmeric powder
1 green chilli, finely chopped

½ tsp Eno's fruit salt

Oil as required, for pan frying

For the kadhi

½ cup gram flour

1 cup curd

3 cups water

1 tsp turmeric powder

½ tsp red chilli powder

½ tsp coriander powder

½ tsp garam masala powder

1 pinch asafoetida

Salt to taste

A handful of coriander leaves, finely chopped

For the seasoning

1 tbsp ghee

½ tsp mustard seeds

¼ tsp cumin seeds

1 inch cinnamon stick, broken

2 red chillies, broken

1 sprig curry leaves

Method

Combine all the ingredients for the palak pakora in a large bowl. Add water, only if required, for a smooth consistency. You can either deep fry or pan fry the pakora.

To deep fry

Preheat the oil over medium heat and add a few tablespoons of the palak pakora mixture at a time and deep fry them until they are golden and crisp. Drain and keep aside.

To make the pakora in a paniyaram pan

Preheat the pan on medium heat. Add a little oil into each cavity and a spoonful of the pakora batter per cavity. Cover the pan and steam the pakoras until you notice that the top part is cooked through and does not look raw.

Next, flip them over to cook them on the other side. Continue to cook on medium heat until the pakoras are cooked from the inside and are golden brown on the outside. Repeat the process for the remaining pakora batter. Keep the pakoras aside.

Next, to make the kadhi, in a large saucepan, whisk the curd, gram flour, asafoetida, chilli powder, turmeric powder, coriander powder, garam masala powder and salt until well blended. Add 3 cups of water and continue to whisk the mixture until well combined.

Place the saucepan over high heat. Keep whisking continuously while the kadhi is on the heat as this will help transform the curd, spices and gram flour into a creamy texture and will prevent it from curdling. Bring the kadhi to a brisk boil for 3 to 4 minutes. Turn the heat to low and simmer for 10 to 15 minutes.

The simmering process helps deepen the flavour of the kadhi and also allows it to thicken slightly—when it's done, it will have a smooth, creamy consistency with a shine to it.

Towards the end of the simmering process, add in the spinach pakora.

Heat the ghee in a tadka pan over medium heat. Add the cumin seeds, mustard seeds, cinnamon stick and the broken red chillies and allow them to splutter.

Finally, stir in the curry leaves and pour the seasoning mixture into the simmering kadhi.

Note: *The kadhi will thicken as the pakora simmers in the curry, so adjust the thickness of the gravy by adding water as required to adjust the consistency.*

Check the salt and spice levels and adjust them to suit your taste. Transfer to a serving bowl, garnish with chopped coriander leaves and serve hot.

∿

Bharwa Karela Masala

This is a great example of transforming a bitter vegetable into a lip-smacking dish. In this recipe, karela (bitter gourd) is stuffed with a potato and paneer mixture and then cooked in a makhani gravy. You can serve it with phulkas and jeera rice for a simple lunch.

Ingredients

For the bharwa karela

3 karela (bitter gourd)
½ cup paneer, grated
2 potatoes, boiled and mashed
Salt to taste
½ tsp black pepper powder
4 sprig coriander leaves, finely chopped
4 sprig mint leaves, finely chopped
Oil for cooking

For the makhani gravy

1 tsp oil
2 onions, finely chopped
2 cups tomato puree
1-inch ginger, finely chopped
4 cloves garlic, finely chopped
2 green chillies, finely chopped
1 tsp Kashmiri red chilli powder
½ tsp coriander powder
½ tsp cumin powder
½ tsp garam masala powder
1 tsp jaggery
3 tbsp fresh cream
Salt to taste
1 tbsp kasuri methi

Method

Peel a very thin outer portion of the rough skin from the bitter gourd without touching the fleshy white inside of the gourd. Keep a layer of the green skin as it is packed with nutrition.

Cut the karela into three cylinders of approximately 1½ to 2 inches. Gently scoop out the flesh and seeds in a way that you are left with only the hollow cylinders of the karela pieces.

In a pressure cooker, add the karela pieces and two tablespoons of water and pressure cook on high heat for 1 whistle. Turn off the heat and release the pressure immediately so that the karela does not get overcooked and it retains a firm texture. Keep aside.

In a mixing bowl, combine the grated paneer, mashed potatoes, salt, pepper, coriander and mint leaves. Mix well. Check the salt and adjust it to suit your taste. Stuff the mixture generously into the karela cylinders.

Heat a few tablespoons of oil in a pan over medium heat. Place the stuffed karela and pan fry until slightly roasted and golden brown all over. Be sure to turn them around from time to time. It will take 5 to 7 minutes to be completely cooked. Once done, keep this aside.

Next, make the gravy. Heat the oil in a saucepan over medium heat. Add the ginger, garlic and onions and sauté them till the onions turn soft and light brown.

Stir in the green chillies, tomato puree, red chilli powder, coriander powder, cumin powder, garam masala powder, jaggery and salt. Bring the gravy to a brisk boil for 3 to 4 minutes.

Turn the heat to low and stir in the cream. Once the cream is well combined, stir in the kasuri methi and turn off the heat.

Arrange the bharwa karela on a serving plate, then pour the makhani gravy over it. Serve hot.

❧

Kala Chana Salad

Here's a high protein salad that you can include in your daily meals. This lip-smacking medley of chopped cucumber, tomato, kala chana (black chickpeas), lemon juice and green chillies also makes a great starter on a hot summer evening.

Ingredients

1 cup kala chana (black chickpeas), soaked for 8 hours or overnight
1 cucumber, finely chopped
2 tomatoes, finely chopped
2 green chillies, finely chopped
1 tsp chaat masala powder
½ tsp roasted cumin powder
Salt to taste
A handful of coriander leaves, finely chopped
Juice from 1 lemon

Method

In a pressure cooker, add the kala chana, a little salt, add the soaked kala chana along with more water such that there is at least 2 inches of water above the chana. Cook on high heat for 3 to 4 whistles. After the whistles, turn the heat to low and simmer for 20 minutes. Then, turn off the heat and allow the pressure to release naturally.

Drain the excess water from the chana and allow it to cool completely. You can use the extra water to cook a dal or soup.

In a large mixing bowl, add the cooked kala chana, chopped cucumber, chopped tomatoes, green chillies, salt, cumin powder, chaat masala powder, coriander leaves and the juice of one lemon.

Stir well to combine and serve chilled.

MEAL PLAN 29

What's on the Plate?

- Hariyali Gobi (Spinach Cauliflower Curry)
- Methi Kadhi (Fenugreek Leaves Yogurt Curry)
- Vegetable Tehri (Pulao with Whole Spices)

- Rajma Salad (Kidney Bean Salad)
- Jowar Atta Roti (Sorghum Flatbread; p. 152)
- Aam Ras (Fresh Mango Pulp; p. 157)

When I put this meal together, I was so pleasantly surprised with the complementary flavours of cauliflower in a palak gravy— instead of the usual paneer—that I decided to serve it with a kadhi, pulao and a high protein rajma salad. And when I plated these dishes together, the food looked bright and colourful—and ended up being lip-smackingly tasty meal. When mangoes are not in season, go ahead and substitute it with a shrikand or a halwa to make the meal festive.

∾

Hariyali Gobi

Making palak paneer at home is a ritual. One day, as I was about to start making this dish, I realized that I had run out of paneer. I decided to use cauliflower instead and was utterly surprised by the result. Here's my recipe for a creamy and spicy hariyali gobi which makes the perfect dish to eat with phulkas for dinner.

Tip: *When you have many dishes like this on your plate, ensure you eat mindfully in the right and small portions.*

Ingredients

For the cauliflower

2 cups cauliflower florets
½ tsp turmeric powder
1 bay leaf, torn into half
1 tsp garam masala powder
Salt to taste
Oil for cooking

For the hariyali masala

500 gm spinach, washed and chopped
1 tomato, finely chopped
2 cloves garlic, finely chopped
2-inch ginger, finely chopped
2 green chillies, finely chopped
½ tsp cumin seeds
1-inch cinnamon stick, broken
1 bay leaf, torn
½ tsp cumin powder
1 tsp garam masala powder
3 tbsp fresh cream
1 tbsp butter
Salt to taste

Method

Heat the butter in a pressure cooker over medium heat. Add the cumin seeds, garlic, ginger and green chillies and sauté them for a few seconds.

Add the cinnamon, tomato, chopped spinach, cumin powder, garam masala powder and salt and sauté together for a few seconds. Next, add a tablespoon of water and pressure cook on high heat for 1 whistle and turn off the heat. Release the pressure immediately to prevent the discoloration of the spinach.

Allow the spinach mixture to cool completely. Then, add it to a blender and make a puree. Keep aside.

Heat the oil in a kadai over medium heat. Add the chopped cauliflower, bay leaf, turmeric powder and salt and sauté for a few seconds. Then, sprinkle a little water and cover the pan. Cook the cauliflower for around 5 minutes.

Once the cauliflower is cooked, toss in the garam masala and stir fry for a few minutes, and then turn off the heat. The cauliflower should be cooked through but still have a firm bite to it. Keep aside.

In a saucepan, add the pureéd spinach mixture, stir in the cream and place the saucepan over high heat. Bring the mixture to a brisk boil. Check the salt and seasonings and adjust them to your taste.

Transfer the spinach gravy to a serving bowl, gently stir in the cooked cauliflower and serve hot.

Methi Kadhi

Methi kadhi is the easiest and simplest curry to whip up to make a comforting meal. This kadhi is made with a mix of curd and besan simmered with fresh methi leaves and a ghee tadka. You can serve this kadhi with a simple jeera pulao and a karela aloo stir fry for a quick meal.

Ingredients

For the kadhi

1 cup curd
¼ cup gram flour
½ tsp turmeric powder
½ tsp coriander powder
½ tsp red chilli powder
2½ cups water
Salt to taste
½ cup methi leaves, washed and chopped
1 onion, thinly sliced
1 tbsp ghee

For the seasoning

1½ tbsp ghee
¼ tsp cumin seeds
¼ mustard seeds
2 dry red chillies, broken

Method

In a large saucepan, combine the gram flour, curd, turmeric powder, coriander powder, red chilli powder and salt. Mix well until smooth.

Add the 2½ cups of water and whisk until it forms a smooth mixture without any lumps. Place the saucepan over medium heat and bring the kadhi to a boil.

While the kadhi is boiling, keep whisking it continuously to ensure a smooth texture. Continue to whisk till you notice that the kadhi has begun to thicken and the texture is smooth. At this stage, turn the heat to low and simmer the kadhi while you get the remaining ingredients ready.

Heat the ghee in a pan over medium heat. Add the sliced onions and sauté them until they turn soft, tender and slightly brown.

Once tender, add in the methi leaves and sauté until they wilt. Once done, turn off the heat.

Stir the onion and methi mixture into the simmering kadhi. Turn the heat to medium so that the kadhi comes to a brisk boil. Let it boil for 3 to 4 minutes, stirring occasionally. Turn the heat to low and simmer for a few more minutes.

While the kadhi is simmering, heat the ghee for the seasoning in a tadka pan over medium heat. Add the mustard seeds and cumin seeds and allow them to splutter. Then, add in the red chillies and stir fry until the chillies are well roasted.

Pour the seasoning over the simmering kadhi. Give it a stir, check the salt and spices and adjust them to suit your taste. Once done, turn off the heat, transfer the kadhi to a serving bowl and serve hot.

Vegetable Tehri

Tehri is a traditional and staple one-pot vegetarian dish from eastern Uttar Pradesh where rice is cooked with whole spices and vegetables, similar to a biryani. You can serve it as a one-pot meal along with raita or kadhi for a quick lunch or dinner.

Ingredients

1½ cups basmati rice, washed
2 cups water

3 tbsp ghee
4 cloves
1-inch cinnamon stick, broken
1 tbsp whole black peppercorns
2 brown cardamom (badi elaichi)
1 bay leaf, torn
1 dry red chilli
1 onion, thinly sliced
1 tomato, finely chopped
1 carrot, chopped
¼ cup green peas, steamed
¼ cup mint leaves, finely chopped
Salt to taste

Method

Heat two tablespoons of ghee in a large saucepan over medium heat. Stir in the cloves, cinnamon stick, black pepper, badi elaichi, bay leaf and red chilli. Sauté these for 2 minutes until you can smell the aromas of the spices.

Stir in the sliced onion and sauté it on low heat for 4 to 5 minutes till it begins to soften and turns slightly brown. Once soft, stir in the tomato and cook until it becomes slightly soft and mushy.

Stir in the peas, carrot, washed rice and salt. Add 2 cups of water and bring the tehri to a brisk boil.

Once it comes to a boil, turn the heat to low, cover the pan and simmer until all the water is absorbed and the rice is cooked. This will take approximately 15 to 20 minutes. Then, turn off the heat and allow the tehri to rest in the pan for 10 minutes.

Open the pan, stir in the mint leaves and a tablespoon of ghee and gently fluff up the tehri. Serve warm.

೧

Rajma Salad

Here is a high protein rajma salad with a fabulous crunch factor that can work both as a side dish or as an evening snack.

Ingredients

1 cup rajma, soaked in water for 8 hours
1 onion, finely chopped
1 tomato, finely chopped
2 green chillies, finely chopped
1 tsp chaat masala powder
½ tsp roasted cumin powder
Juice from 1 lemon
A handful of mint leaves, finely chopped
Salt to taste

Method

In a pressure cooker, add the soaked rajma along with its water, a dash of salt and some more water such that it is at least 2 inches above the rajma and cook on high heat for 4 to 5 whistles. Then, turn the heat to low and simmer for another 20 minutes and turn off the heat. Allow the pressure to release naturally. The rajma should be soft inside and fully cooked. Drain the excess water, then keep the rajma aside and allow it to cool.

In a mixing bowl, add the cooled rajma, onion, tomato, green chillies, chaat masala powder, cumin powder, salt, mint leaves and lemon juice.

Mix well to combine the rajma salad. Check the salt and adjust it to your taste. Serve chilled.

MEAL PLAN 30

What's on the Plate?

- Muttakose Kootu (Cabbage Lentil Stew)
- Vazhaipoo Poriyal (Banana Flower Stir Fry)
- Kathrikai Poondu Piratal (Brinjal Garlic Stir Fry)

- Thakkali Poondu Rasam (Spicy Tomato Garlic Soup)
- Paruppu Payasam (Jaggery Lentil Pudding)
- Curd
- Rice
- Appalam

Here is an authentic meal from Tamil Nadu which has a blend of stir fry vegetables like vazhaipoo poriyal, which is made with the flower of the banana tree, kathirikai poondu piratal, which is a classic brinjal stir fry, and a high protein cabbage kootu served with rasam and rice. An elaborate meal like this is often made during festivals like Tamil New Year or even for a special occasion in the family, but you can also whip this up for a special Sunday lunch when you have family and friends over.

Tip: Do ensure you portion your meal and eat mindfully

Muttakoose Kootu

Easy to make and very healthy, this cabbage kootu is a wholesome and high protein dish in which moong dal is cooked with steamed cabbage and a fresh coconut masala, then finished off with a crunchy tadka.

Ingredients

2 cups cabbage, roughly chopped
1 cup yellow split moong dal
½ tsp turmeric powder
Salt to taste

To be ground

½ cup fresh coconut, in pieces
2 tsp cumin seeds
2 tsp whole black peppercorns
¼ cup warm water

For the seasoning

½ tsp mustard seeds
1 tsp white urad dal
1 sprig curry leaves
1 tsp coconut oil

Method

In a pressure cooker, add the chopped cabbage, 2 tablespoons of water and salt and pressure cook on high heat for 1 whistle. Turn off the heat and release the pressure immediately. This will prevent the cabbage from getting overcooked. Transfer this to a bowl and keep it aside.

In the same pressure cooker, add the washed moong dal with turmeric powder and 1 cup of water. Pressure cook on high heat for 2 to 3 whistles. After the whistles, turn off the heat, allow the pressure to release naturally and keep it aside.

In a mixer grinder, add the grated coconut, cumin seeds and black peppercorns with ¼ cup of warm water and grind to a smooth paste. Keep aside. This is the kootu masala.

Add the cabbage and coconut masala to the pressure-cooked moong dal and give it a quick stir. Add salt to taste and bring the kootu a brisk boil, then turn off the heat. Taste the dish and adjust the salt and seasonings accordingly.

Transfer the muttakoose kootu to a serving bowl.

Finally, heat one teaspoon of coconut oil in a small tadka pan over medium heat; add the mustard seeds and urad dal and let the seeds splutter. Allow the dal to turn golden brown and crisp. Stir in the curry leaves for about 10 seconds and turn off the heat.

Pour this tadka over the prepared kootu and give it a stir and serve hot.

Vazhaipoo Poriyal

Another wholesome and delicious south Indian stir fry made with banana flower tossed in grated coconut, green chillies and a crunchy tadka of curry leaves. It makes a perfect high fibre, vitamin- and mineral-rich side dish which you can also serve with phulkas and dal.

Ingredients

1 banana flower
3 tbsp curd
1 tsp coconut oil
1 tsp mustard seeds
1½ tsp white urad dal
10 pearl onions (sambar onions), finely chopped
2 green chillies, finely chopped
2 sprig curry leaves, roughly chopped
½ tsp turmeric powder
¼ cup fresh coconut, grated
Salt to taste

Method

In a bowl, add 3 cups water and 3 tablespoons of curd and a little salt to make a buttermilk mixture. Mix well.

To prune the banana flower, grease your fingers and palms with oil so that the vegetable does not darken your nails and hands.

Separate the edible flower part, which looks whitish-yellow, by removing the purple petals one by one. The next step is to remove the middle bud/stem from the flower. You will find the two parts of the flower. Remove the one which is pointed; these don't cook well.

Once done, place the banana flower in the chaas. This step stops the banana flower from turning dark. Once you have pruned all the flowers, you can chop them. Discard the water.

Ensure the remaining ingredients are ready as well.

Heat one teaspoon of coconut oil in a pan over medium heat. Add the mustard seeds and urad dal and allow the seeds to splutter and the dal to turn crisp and golden brown.

Once done, stir in the curry leaves, green chillies and the chopped pearl onions. Sauté till the onions are soft.

Next, add the coconut, turmeric powder and the chopped banana flower. You can add a few tablespoons of the buttermilk water, then add salt to taste and cover the pan. Cook the banana flower for about ten minutes until it is soft.

Once the banana flower is cooked, remove the lid and stir fry so that any excess water can evaporate. Check the salt and adjust it according to your taste. Turn off the heat and transfer to a bowl and serve hot.

Kathrikai Poondu Piratal

Kathirikai poondu pirattal is a specialty of the Chettinad region of Tamil Nadu. A simple brinjal stir fry flavoured with garlic and a freshly roasted and ground spice mix, this dish is usually served with hot steamed rice, parotta and spicy onion kuzhambu. In this recipe, I have used sambar powder, which adds a special flavour to the dish.

Ingredients

500 gm long green brinjal, cut into long strips
1 onion, finely chopped
12 cloves garlic, crushed
1 tomato, finely chopped
½ tsp turmeric powder
1 tbsp sambar powder
Salt to taste
2 tbsp of sunflower or sesame oil
1 tsp mustard seeds
1 tsp white split urad dal
½ tsp asafoetida
1 sprig curry leaves, torn
2 dry red chillies, broken into half

Method

Cut the brinjal vertically and place it in a bowl filled with salt water to avoid darkening.

Heat the oil in a heavy-bottomed pan over medium heat. Add the mustard seeds and urad dal and allow the seeds to splutter and the dal to turn golden brown and crisp.

Add the asafoetida, curry leaves and dried red chillies and allow them to roast for a few seconds.

Next, add the garlic and onion and sauté until the onion turns soft and change colour. This will take about 2 to 3 minutes.

Once done, add the tomato and the brinjals, and season the dish with salt.

Sprinkle some water over the brinjals, cover the pan and cook the dish on low heat. This will take around 10 minutes.

Once the brinjals are cooked, add the turmeric powder and sambar powder and stir well.

Stir fry the kathirikai poondu pirattal for another 3 to 4 minutes, stirring in between. Check the salt and seasonings and adjust them according to your taste, then turn off the heat.

Transfer to a serving bowl and serve hot.

Tomato Garlic Rasam

This classic south Indian rasam is simple, comforting and perfect for chilly winter evenings when all you want is something warm and spicy. You can have it as a warm soup during cold weather.

Ingredients

For the rasam

¼ cup toor dal
1 tsp turmeric powder
20 gm tamarind, soaked in hot water for 10 minutes
5 tomatoes, roughly chopped
1 tbsp ghee
½ tsp roasted cumin powder
¼ tsp asafoetida
½ tsp roasted coriander powder
½ tsp black pepper powder
¼ tsp red chilli powder
Salt to taste

A handful of coriander leaves, finely chopped

For the seasoning

1 tbsp ghee
4 cloves garlic, crushed
4 curry leaves
¼ tsp mustard seeds
¼ tsp cumin seeds

Method

To make the tamarind water, after 10 minutes of soaking, use your fingers to mash the tamarind well into the water until it feels completely soft. This process helps to extract the juice and sourness from the tamarind.

Next, strain the tamarind water into a fresh bowl and squeeze out as much extract from the pulp as possible.

Next we will proceed to the second extraction of the remaining tamarind pulp. Add another 1/2 cup of water and mash the pulp once again to make more tamarind water.

Strain this second extract over the earlier one and keep aside.

In a pressure cooker, add the toor dal with 1 cup of water and pressure cook it on high heat for 2 whistles. After the whistles, turn the heat to low and simmer for 5 minutes, then turn off the heat. Allow the pressure to release naturally. Once the pressure has released, mash the dal well until smooth. Keep aside.

Pureé the cut tomatoes in a blender and keep aside.

Heat the ghee in a saucepan over medium heat; add the mustard seeds, cumin seeds, garlic and curry leaves.

When the mustard seeds begin to splutter, pour in the tomato puree, cooked dal, tamarind water, coriander powder, turmeric powder, cumin powder, asafoetida, black pepper and red chilli powder.

Stir well to combine and bring the rasam to a brisk boil for 2 to 3 minutes. Then, simmer the rasam for 10 minutes on low heat until you see it frothing. When you notice it frothing, turn off the heat. Check the salt and seasonings and adjust them according to your taste.

Finally, garnish with freshly chopped coriander leaves and serve hot.

Paruppu Payasam

Here's a recipe that debunks the myth that desserts are bad for us. This payasam recipe features the high protein green moong dal cooked in coconut milk, flavoured with cardamom powder and sweetened with jaggery, and finally, served with cashewnuts fried in ghee.

Ingredients

1 cup whole green moong dal, soaked in warm water for 2 hours
½ cup jaggery
¼ cup water
1 tsp cardamom powder
1 cup coconut milk
A pinch of saffron strands
1 tbsp ghee
½ cup broken cashew nuts

Method

In a pressure cooker, add the soaked green moong dal along with the water such that there is at least 1 inch of water above the dal. Cook the dal on high heat for 3 whistles.

After the whistles, turn the heat to low and simmer for 5 minutes, and then turn off the heat. Allow the pressure to release naturally. Keep aside.

Heat a saucepan on medium heat. Combine the jaggery with ¼ cup of water so that the jaggery melts. Bring this syrup to a brisk boil.

Reduce the heat, add the cooked green moong dal, coconut milk, saffron strands and cardamom powder and simmer for 5 minutes until the flavours have seeped into the payasam.

Next, heat a small tadka pan over low heat, add the ghee and fry the cashewnuts until they are golden brown and crisp.

Stir the roasted cashews into the payasam and serve hot or chilled.

ACCOMPANIMENTS

Amla Pickle

Ingredients

100 gm gooseberries (amla), deseeded and finely chopped
1 tsp methi seeds, roasted and powdered
1 tsp mustard seeds
1 tsp mustard oil
1 tsp red chilli powder
½ tsp turmeric powder
½ tsp asafoetida
Salt to taste

Method

Heat the oil in a small skillet over medium heat. Add the mustard seeds and allow them to splutter. Stir in the asafoetida, turmeric powder, powered methi seeds and red chilli powder.

Cut the gooseberries and place them in a mixing bowl. Pour the seasoning over the cut berries, add the salt to taste and give it a good stir.

Store the pickle in a glass jar and refrigerate for a month. Serve this as an accompaniment with your meals.

❧

Instant Raw Mango Pickle

Ingredients

1 raw mango, peeled and finely chopped
1 tsp red chilli powder
¼ tsp methi kuria
½ tsp rai kuria
¼ tsp turmeric powder
¼ tsp asafoetida
1 tbsp mustard oil
Salt to taste

Method

Combine all the ingredients in a bowl. Stir until everything is well combined.

Store the instant raw mango pickle in a glass bottle and refrigerate it for a month.

Serve this pickle with dals, parathas, rice—or just about any meal that could do with an extra bit of flavour.

Turmeric Pickle

Ingredients

100 gm fresh turmeric root
50 gm ginger
1 tbsp mustard seeds
2 tbsp lemon juice
1 tsp mustard oil
Salt to taste

Method

In a skillet on medium heat, roast the mustard seeds until they start to splutter. Allow the seeds to cool a bit, and then blend to make a coarse powder. Keep aside.

Peel the turmeric and ginger and julienne them, that is, cut them into thin strips.

In a large mixing bowl, combine the turmeric, ginger, mustard powder, salt and oil.

Squeeze fresh lemon juice on to this and adjust the amount of lemon juice as needed. Mix well and transfer the pickle into a bottle.

Refrigerate the pickle and allow it to marinate in the fridge for a day before serving. The pickle will stay refrigerated for a month.

Green Chilli Pickle

250 gm green chillies, chopped
¼ cup mustard seeds
2 tbsp fenugreek seeds
3 tbsp rock salt (sendha namak)
2 tsp turmeric powder
½ cup mustard oil
juice from 5 lemons

Method

Wash the green chillies and wipe them cleam. Keep it in the open air for a few hours. There should be no trace of moisture.

Remove the stem and chop the green chillies into 1 inch size pieces. Place it in a steel or glass mixing bowl.

Add the mustard seeds and fenugreek seeds to a blender and make a coarse powder.

Add the salt, mustard and fenugreek seed powder, lemon juice and mustard oil to the chopped green chillies.

Mix well to combine. Check the salt; it should be very salty. If it is not salty, add a teaspoon of salt more at a time and mix until very salty. Cover the bowl with a muslin cloth and then a steel lid.

Allow the pickle to marinate for 3 to 4 days and keep stirring it twice a day. You will notice the green chillies softening and attaining a pickle-like consistency.

Once you notice that the pickling process is complete, transfer to a glass jar and store and use as required.

Note: *the pickle will continue to marinate and become softer over time.*

Beetroot Raita

Ingredients

2 cups plain curd
1 raw beetroot, finely grated
2 green chillies, finely chopped
1 tsp cumin powder
Salt to taste
For the seasoning
½ tsp sunflower oil
¼ tsp mustard seeds
½ tsp white urad dal
1 sprig curry leaves

Method

In a large mixing bowl, add the curd, salt, cumin powder, green chillies and grated beetroot. Whisk well to combine. Check the salt and spice levels and adjust them to suit your taste. Transfer the raita to a serving bowl.

Next, make the seasoning.

Heat the oil in a tadka pan over medium heat. Add the mustard seeds and urad dal and allow the seeds to splutter and the dal to turn golden brown and crisp.

Finally, stir in the curry leaves and turn off the heat.

Pour the seasoning onto the beetroot raita and serve fresh.

Boondi Raita

Ingredients

½ cup boondi
2 cups plain curd
½ tsp chaat masala powder
¼ tsp kala namak (black salt)
¼ tsp roasted cumin powder
¼ tsp red chilli powder
Salt to taste

Method

In a mixing bowl, add the curd, red chilli powder, chaat masala powder, kala namak, cumin powder and salt.

Add 2 or 3 tablespoons of water and whisk until smooth. Gently fold the boondi into the whisked curd.

Check the salt and seasonings and adjust them to suit your taste.

Transfer the boondi raita to a serving bowl and garnish with chopped coriander leaves. Serve chilled.

Burani Raita

Ingredients

1½ cups plain curd
4 cloves garlic, finely chopped
½ tsp roasted cumin powder
½ tsp red chilli powder
½ tsp kala namak
Salt to taste

Method

In a large mixing bowl, add the curd, garlic, red chilli powder, cumin powder and kala namak.

Whisk well to combine until smooth. Check the salt and adjust it according to your taste.

Serve chilled with your favourite meal.

∾

Tomato Onion Cucumber Raita

Ingredients

2 cups plain curd
1 cucumber, finely chopped
1 tomato, finely chopped
1 onion, finely chopped
2 green chillies, finely chopped
½ tsp cumin powder
Salt to taste

Method

In a bowl, add the curd and whisk well. Add the salt and cumin powder and add all the chopped vegetables and give it a stir.

Transfer to a serving bowl. Serve chilled with biryanis, parathas or any other meal of your choice.

∾

Carrot Peanut Salad

Ingredients

2 carrots, grated
1 cucumber, peeled and finely chopped
1 tomato, finely chopped
1 green chilli, finely chopped
¼ cup halved roasted peanuts
Juice from 1 lemon

1 tsp honey

A handful of coriander leaves, finely chopped

Method

In a mixing bowl, combine the carrots, cucumber, tomato, green chilli, roasted peanuts, lemon juice, honey and coriander leaves.

Toss the salad well and serve immediately.

Manga Pachadi

Ingredients

2 mangoes (raw), peeled and cut into small chunks

½ cup jaggery, powdered

¼ tsp red chilli powder

¼ tsp turmeric powder

1 tsp salt

½ cup water

For the seasoning

½ tsp mustard seeds

½ tsp cumin seeds

1 sprig curry leaves, torn

2 dry red chillies, broken into halves

1 tbsp sesame oil

Method

Add the raw mango into the pressure cooker, along with jaggery, salt, turmeric powder and red chilli powder. Add ½ cup of water and pressure cook on high heat for 3 whistles and turn off the heat.

Allow the pressure to release naturally. Once done, open the cooker and you will notice the manga pachadi having a jam-like consistency.

Give it a stir and taste it. Add more salt if required.

Next, make the seasoning. Heat the oil in a pan over medium heat; add the mustard seeds, cumin seeds and red chillies. Stir until the seeds crackle and the chillies are lightly roasted.

Add the curry leaves, and then stir in the cooked mango mixture.

Bring it to a brisk boil and turn off the heat. Transfer the pachadi to a serving bowl or store it in an airtight container.

The pachadi will stay for at least one week when refrigerated.

Jeera Rice

Ingredients

1 cup rice, washed
2 tsp cumin seeds
2 green chillies, slit
2 tbsp ghee, divided
Salt to taste

Method

Place the washed rice in a saucepan and add salt, 1 tablespoon of the ghee and two cups of water.

On high heat, bring the rice to a brisk boil. Then, cover the pan, turn the heat to low and cook the rice till all the water is completely absorbed. This should take about 15 to 20 minutes. Turn off the heat.

Allow the rice to rest with the lid on for 10 minutes. The rice will fluff up as it rests.

Heat the remaining tablespoon of ghee in a small pan over medium heat. Add the cumin seeds and green chillies and allow the cumin to splutter and the green chillies to roast till you can see that its skin has shrunk a little. When you can smell the roasted aroma of the seasoning, turn off the heat.

Pour the roasted cumin and green chillies into the cooked rice. Using a slotted spoon, stir the rice gently and fluff it up.

Serve warm with your favourite dal or sabzi.

Jowar/Ragi Atta Roti

Ingredients

½ cup jowar flour or ragi flour
1½ cups whole wheat flour
1 tsp black pepper powder
Salt to taste
1 tbsp oil

Method

In a large mixing bowl, add the jowar/ragi flour, whole wheat flour, salt and pepper to taste. Add water a little at a time and knead to make a smooth dough.

Drizzle 1 teaspoon of oil and knead until the dough comes away from the sides of the pan and is smooth.

Divide the dough into lemon-size portions. Take a portion of the dough and dust it in wheat flour. Roll the dough into a 5- to 6-inch diameter circle.

On a preheated skillet, place the rolled-out dough and cook for a few seconds on medium-high heat until small bubbles appear on the surface of the roti.

Flip and cook the roti for a few seconds, then place it over the open flame. Flip the roti on the flame and allow it to puff up. If it does not puff up, flip and turn it until brown spots appear on both sides and the roti is cooked.

Once done, transfer the roti onto a serving plate and smear a little ghee on it. Serve immediately.

Bajra Na Rotla

Ingredients

1 cup bajra flour (Pearl Millet)
Salt to taste
Water as required

Note: You will also need a wet muslin cloth. A cotton white handkerchief will also work well.

In a wide bowl, combine the flour and salt; add water, a little at a time, to make a stiff dough. Cover the dough and allow it to rest for 10 minutes. Knead once again and divide the dough into 6 portions. Preheat your iron skillet on medium heat.

Traditionally, this rolta is cooked on a clay skillet, if you do have one, go ahead and use it. But for all practical purposes the iron skillet works just as well.

Using wet palms place the ball on the wet muslin cloth and flatten the ball with your palms. Continue pressing the dough until the rotla has attained a round shape. If you find any cracks, use your finger to pinch the cracks together and seal them.

Invert the rotla on the heated iron skillet and cook for about 40 secconds on medium heat and turn over gently with a flat spatula to the other side.

Turn the heat to low and allow the rotla to cook slowly. Once again flip and cook on low heat until well done and you notice light golden spots. You will notice that it begins to puff when it is cooking slowly on low heat. There are times the rotla will not puff; so don't get hassled, just allow it to cook evenly and you can still savour it. Continue the process with the remaining portions of the dough. Turn off the heat.

Serve the bajra rotla hot with jaggery and butter or ringna no olo. Bajra na rotla has to be served straight from the stove; if it cools down, it will feel very dry and bland. There are a few things which have to come straight from the stove to the plate and this is one of them.

❧

Tawa Paratha

Ingredients

1½ cups whole wheat flour
½ tsp salt
1 tsp oil
Ghee for cooking

Method

In a large bowl, combine the flour and salt. Knead this into a dough, adding a little water at a time, to make the dough smooth.

Add one tablespoon of oil and knead it again to make the dough smooth. Divide the dough into 10 portions.

Preheat an iron skillet on medium heat.

Roll the dough into balls and flatten them with the palm of your hand. Toss them in flour and roll them out into circles of approximately 3 inches diameter.

We need to get a triangle shape. To do so, fold the rolled out dough into a semi-circle, then fold the semi-circle into half again. You will get a mini triangle shape.

Tossing the triangle in a little flour, roll it out gently into a larger triangle to make it thinner. Repeat the process with the remaining dough portions.

With the skillet on medium heat, place the rolled-out paratha dough on the skillet. After a few seconds, you will notice air pockets on its surface.

Flip the paratha and smear half a teaspoon of ghee on its surface. Using a flat spatula, press lightly and turn the paratha to cook it.

Flip the paratha and repeat the process. When you notice brown spots on the paratha and it is slightly crisp, remove it from the heat and place it on a platter. Serve hot.

❧

Puri

Ingredients

2 cups whole wheat flour
2 tsp oil
Salt to taste
Oil for deep frying

Method

In a large bowl, combine the flour and salt together and then add the 2 teaspoons of oil. Add water, a little at a time, and knead well to make a firm and smooth dough.

Add another teaspoon of oil to smoothen the dough further and knead again. Divide the dough into 20 equal portions.

Heat oil in a deep-frying pan over medium heat. Using a rolling pin, roll out each ball into a 5-inch diameter circle, sprinkling a little oil while rolling to prevent the dough from sticking to the base.

When the oil is hot, gently slip in a single rolled-out dough. Using a slotted spatula, fry the puri, continuously yet gently pouring oil onto the puri and allowing it to puff up.

Once the puri puffs up, turn it over and fry the other side for a few seconds. Using the slotted spatula, lift the puri and drain the oil by the side of the pan.

Place the fried puri on a paper towel to absorb any excess oil. Repeat the process with the remaining dough. Serve hot.

∾

Lacha Pyaz

Ingredients

2 onions, thinly sliced into rings
Juice from 1 lemon
Black salt (kala namak) as required

¼ tsp red chilli powder (optional)
¼ tsp chaat masala powder (optional)
Salt to taste

Method

In a mixing bowl, add the onion rings, lemon juice and black salt to taste. You can add the red chilli powder and chaat masala powder to make the flavour of the lacha pyaz more chatpata. Mix well.

Cover the bowl and allow the onions to marinate for 15 to 20 minutes.

Serve the lacha pyaz with your favourite meal.

∾

Lassi

Ingredients

1 cup plain curd
2 tbsp sugar or honey
¼ cup fresh cream
3 to 4 saffron strands (optional)
A few ice cubes

Method

In a blender, add the curd, saffron, cream and sugar to make a smooth lassi. Serve chilled with ice cubes.

You can also add chopped pistachios or even rose water to give the lassi a different flavour.

∾

Chaas

Ingredients

1 cup plain curd/yogurt
2 cups water
1 green chilli, chopped
Pinch of salt (optional)

Method

Add the curd, salt, green chilli and some water to a blender.

Blend to make a chaas and serve chilled.

You can also add an inch of ginger, a sprig of curry leaf and a pinch of asafoetida to add a variation to this chaas.

Aam Ras

Ingredients

3 cups ripe mango
¼ cup water
2 tbsp sugar (optional)

Method

Roll the whole mangoes with your palms to soften them.

Peel the mango, roughly chop and transfer all the pulp into a mixer jar, discarding the seed.

Add water and sugar to suit your taste depending on the sweetness of the mango.

Blend until smooth. The aam ras is now ready. Refrigerate for a few hours and serve chilled along with your meal.

Jhat Pat Mirchi

Ingredients

5 green chillies
Salt to taste
2 tbsp oil

Method

Make a slit in the green chillies without cutting them into half. The slit will prevent the green chillies from bursting and popping when you are pan frying them.

Heat the oil in a pan over medium heat. Add the green chillies and pan fry them till you notice them starting to shrink. They should also turn soft and start to change colour, and should have small brown spots.

Once done, remove the chillies from the pan, then drain the excess oil from the chillies by placing them on kitchen paper towels. Sprinkle salt and toss well to combine.

Serve with your favourite meal.

Acknowledgements

In no particular order, this book has happened because of:

The fans of Archana's Kitchen, who constantly request recipes across cuisines, ask for meal plans and even what kind of food they can make for special diets for patients. These meal plans would not have seen the light of day without their innumerable requests to help me plan their everyday meals and lunch boxes. Their support and courage have been amazing.

My mom, who taught me the finer skills of healthy cooking, and who made it easy for me to explore various cuisines when we visited friends' homes for dinners or when we travelled across cities. She would often jot down recipes for future use, and cut out recipe clips from various magazines and newspapers and cook those recipes at home. I continue this habit till date—I relish the food that I eat at restaurants and at people's homes. I am constantly trying to decipher the recipes for the food I like and just like my mom, I jot them down and transform them into the recipes which now get published on the Archana's Kitchen website.

My dad, who loved to eat and travel and made my journey towards an independent life and towards food exploration the most joyous ever. We would often sneak out on Sundays and eat a special breakfast at a roadside shop or a biryani at a place he would have discovered. I miss you.

My boys, who are some of my biggest critiques, who can now expertly identify spices based on their aromas when I cook, and who have eaten everything I have placed on their plates—giving me the gratification of deciphering what they enjoyed the most and a better understanding of how to perfect a recipe. I hope you will find this book useful as you venture into your own kitchens to cook meals for your families.

My dear H, who has been my backbone and who has supported me in my journey of building Archana's Kitchen to what it is today—from building and maintaining my website, to ensuring I reply to all the fan queries as quickly as I can, to helping me do the dishes after a long day and to always saying everything tastes awesome. You are the best.

My brother, who is the biggest critic of my recipes. Each time I have written a recipe, he has read and tried cooking the recipe as per the instructions. Each time, he has given me a call and pointed out flaws in the language or the recipe, making me think deeper about how to write recipes in a language that can be understood by all. Thanks bro, for making me dive deeper. I do use all your tips.

To my mother-in-law, who makes legendary Gujarati Jain food, without whom I would not have dared to explore cooking north Indian dishes without onion and garlic, and still make a dish that tastes lip-smacking delicious.

And finally, to my lovely editor, Trisha Bora, Hina Khajuria and the rest of the team at HarperCollins who worked as hard as me to bring life to this book. Thank you.

About the Author

Archana Doshi founded Archana's Kitchen in 2007, and it soon grew into India's leading food and recipe platform. Over two decades later, Archana's Kitchen has more than 10 million users across her website, YouTube channel, social media pages and mobile app. She was featured as 'Google Entrepreneur on the Web' for her outstanding work on the digital space for food and was the inspiration for the first Google Chrome ad on national television in India.